The History of the Kiss!

Semiotics and Popular Culture

Series Editor: Marcel Danesi

Written by leading figures in the interconnected fields of popular culture, media, and semiotic studies, the books in this series aim to show the contemporary relevance of cultural theory. Individual volumes offer an exercise in unraveling the sociopsychological reasons why certain cultural trends become popular. The series engages with theory and technical trends to expose the subject matter clearly, openly, and meaningfully.

Marcel Danesi is professor of Semiotics and Anthropology at the University of Toronto. Among his major publications are *X-Rated!*; *Of Cigarettes, High Heels, and Other Interesting Things; Vico, Metaphor, and the Origins of Language*; *Cool: The Signs and Meanings of Adolescence*; *The Puzzle Instinct: The Meaning of Puzzles in Human Life*; and *Brands*. He is editor in chief of *Semiotica*, the leading journal in semiotics.

The History of the Kiss!
The Birth of Popular Culture

Marcel Danesi

palgrave
macmillan

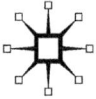

THE HISTORY OF THE KISS!
Copyright © Marcel Danesi, 2013.

Softcover reprint of the hardcover 1st edition 2013 978-1-137-37683-1

All rights reserved.

First published in 2013 by
PALGRAVE MACMILLAN®
in the United States—a division of St. Martin's Press LLC,
175 Fifth Avenue, New York, NY 10010.

Where this book is distributed in the UK, Europe and the rest of the world,
this is by Palgrave Macmillan, a division of Macmillan Publishers Limited,
registered in England, company number 785998, of Houndmills,
Basingstoke, Hampshire RG21 6XS.

Palgrave Macmillan is the global academic imprint of the above companies
and has companies and representatives throughout the world.

Palgrave® and Macmillan® are registered trademarks in the United States,
the United Kingdom, Europe and other countries.

ISBN 978-1-137-37684-8   ISBN 978-1-137-37685-5 (eBook)
DOI 10.1057/9781137376855

Library of Congress Cataloging-in-Publication Data

Danesi, Marcel, 1946–
    The history of the kiss! : the birth of popular culture / by Marcel
Danesi.
        pages cm.—(Semiotics and popular culture)
    Includes bibliographical references and index.

    1. Kissing—History. 2. Kissing—Social aspects. I. Title.

GT2640.D36 2013
394—dc23   2013024735

A catalogue record of the book is available from the British Library.

Design by Newgen Knowledge Works (P) Ltd., Chennai, India.

First edition: December 2013

10 9 8 7 6 5 4 3 2 1

Contents

Figures

Preface

What's more romantic than two people embracing, looking into each other's eyes, and then, to put the final touches on the idyllic moment, kissing each other on the lips? At that instant, the force of gravity seems no longer to be in effect, as the kiss transports the lovers to another plane of existence—high above the mundane. Why is this physical act so meaningful and emotionally powerful? Why does the same kind of lifting experience not come about by touching knees or elbows? What is it about the romantic lip kiss that turns ordinary people into passionate lovers? Is kissing part of human nature, as instinctual to courtship as salivation is to digestion? Or is it something that we have inherited from our past?

This book is an attempt to make sense of the kiss. Unlike current thinking in the human sciences, which tend to ascribe a biological basis to its origins, I will claim that it surfaced in the society of the medieval period as an act of betrayal and carnality, as opposed to the sacred act of breathing into the spouse's mouth as an act of fidelity and spirituality (the exchange of souls through the breath). In that period the romantic lip kiss started appearing in narratives, poetry, and the chansons celebrating the deeds of legendary figures and their love affairs. Romance has not been the same since. Nor have courtship practices. The kiss has since evolved into the ideal symbol of love in the popular imagination, empowering everyone to seek their own romantic destiny, apart from the wishes of family or traditional customs. The origins of the kiss signal the birth of popular culture, or at least of a proto-version of it, and of women's gradual liberation. I will bring some original research to bear on my argument in the final chapter—research asking young people about their interpretations of kissing that was conducted at the University of Toronto between 2009 and 2012. Overall, my claim is that kissing is not imprinted in our genes; rather, it is a product of cultural events that took courtship away from the control of the family, making it a matter of personal choice. The need for love is universal, but the enactment of love is culture specific. Its contemporary form originated in a specific place, at a specific point in time. Because of the electronic global village in which we live, the kiss, like popular culture itself, has spread throughout the world, finding its way into, and changing (or at least upsetting), traditions and practices of romance everywhere.

I was challenged indirectly to write this book by a student in one of my classes at the University of Toronto. I was discussing romantic movies, when the topic of the kiss inevitably came up. At a certain point, a young lady at the back of the class raised her hand and asked: "Why do we experience such an unhygienic act as beautiful and romantic?" I couldn't answer her question on the spot, because I really had no answer. I simply gave her the usual academic evasive comment: "I will get back to you on it." I never did. This book is my response.

We do indeed experience a kiss as something "beautiful," as my student pointed out. It unites the physical, sexual part of lovemaking with the romantic, spiritual part. As the 1950s pop music singer Jimmy Rodgers so aptly put it in his number one hit song, "kisses" are "sweeter than wine." Like a sip of a vintage wine a kiss is pleasurable and intoxicating, leaving us satisfied, but desirous for more, much more. In the end, the story of the kiss is a story of why humans need and seek love and why they need to express it freely. Without it, the world would make no sense, as the famous American dancer, Isadora Duncan, wrote in her uncompleted memoirs: "All that is necessary to make this world a better place to live in is to love."[1]

Series Preface

Popular forms of entertainment have always existed.
As he traveled the world, the ancient Greek historian
Herodotus wrote about earthy, amusing performances
and songs that seemed odd to him, but which were certainly
very popular with common folk. He saw these, however, as
the exception to the rule of true culture. One wonders what
Herodotus would think in today's media culture, where his
"exception" has become the rule. Why is popular culture so
"popular"? What is psychologically behind it? What is it? Why
do we hate to love it and love to hate it? What has happened
to so-called high culture? What are the "meanings" and "social
functions" of current pop culture forms such as sitcoms, reality
TV programs, YouTube sites, and the like?

These are the kinds of questions that this series of books,
written by experts and researchers in both popular culture
studies and semiotics, will broach and discuss critically.
Overall, they will attempt to decode the meanings inherent
in spectacles, popular songs, coffee, video games, cars, fads,
and other "objects" of contemporary pop culture. They will
also take comprehensive glances at the relationship between
culture and the human condition. Although written by scholars and intellectuals, each book will look beyond the many
abstruse theories that have been put forward to explain popular
culture, so as to penetrate its origins, evolution, and overall
raison d'être human life, exploring the psychic structures that
it expresses and which make it so profoundly appealing, even
to those who claim to hate it. Pop culture has been *the* driving

force in guiding, or at leashing shaping, social evolution since the Roaring Twenties, triggering a broad debate about art, sex, and "true culture" that is still ongoing. This debate is a crucial one in today's global village where traditional canons of art and aesthetics are being challenged as never before in human history.

The books are written in clear language and style so that readers of all backgrounds can understand what is going on in pop culture theory and semiotics, and thus reflect upon current cultural trends. They have the dual function of introducing various disciplinary attitudes and research findings in a user-friendly fashion so that they can be used as texts in colleges and universities, while still appealing to the interested general reader. Ultimately, the goal of each book is to provide a part of a generic semiotic framework for understanding the world we live in and probably will live in for the foreseeable future.

Marcel Danesi
University of Toronto

Acknowledgments

I wish to acknowledge the help and support of the following people in the writing of this book. First, I thank my research assistants, all University of Toronto students, who gathered very important and useful information for this project, and who provided me with precious insights of their own. They include: Mariana Bockarova, Vanessa Hall, Justin Commu, Marisa Falconi, Patrick McElcheran, Stacy Costa, Caitlin Grieve, Lorraine Bryers, Vanessa Compagnone, and Chelsea Leigh. I must also thank the administrators at Victoria College for providing the resources I needed to conduct the research, especially David Cook, the ex-principal of the college. Last, but certainly not least, I must thank my lovely and supportive wife, Lucia. She is the ultimate inspiration for this book. I will never forget our first kiss, which, as she knows, was performed under the stars (where else?) on a small island, called Centre Island, just outside downtown Toronto.

CHAPTER 1

The Popular Origins of the Kiss

Give me a thousand kisses, a hundred more, another thousand,
and another hundred.

—Catullus (84–54 BCE)

Romantic love and the act of lip kissing are now so inter-twined in the popular imagination that people hardly ever stop to think not only why we do it, but also why we have developed a worldwide culture of lovemaking revolving around that act. The German language has 30 words refer-ring to different types of kisses, including *Nachkuss*, which means "making up for kisses that have not been given." Some societies, on the other hand, have no words whatsoever for this act, indicating that it is not a part of their courtship rituals, or at least was not in the past. But wherever it is a part, kissing has an enduring and transformative effect, physically, psycho-logically, and socially, regardless of the age, social class, and educational background of the kissers. It has been estimated that, before marrying, the average American woman has kissed 79 men;[1] more than 92 percent of Americans have engaged in kissing before the age of 14; and husbands who kiss their wives on a regular basis apparently live five years longer on average than those who do not.[2]

Some kisses have become so iconic that they have come to emblemize significant episodes in the history of romance. These include the kiss between Romeo and Juliet, Guinevere and Lancelot, and a sailor and a nurse in downtown Manhattan captured in a 1945 *Life* magazine photo by Alfred Eisenstaedt. Many movies are memorable because of a particular kiss performed in them: *Gone with the Wind* (Clark Gable and Vivian Leigh), *From Here to Eternity* (Burt Lancaster and Deborah Kerr), *Rear Window* (James Stewart and Grace Kelly), *An Officer and a Gentleman* (Richard Gere and Debra Winger), and *Titanic* (Leonardo DiCaprio and Kate Winslett), to mention but a few. Kissing is the theme in such classic pop songs as *Kiss of Fire* (Louis Armstrong and Georgia Gibb), *Kiss Me Big* (Tennessee Ernie Ford), *Kisses Sweeter than Wine* (Jimmy Rodgers), *The Shoop Shoop Song* (Betty Everett), *Kisses of Fire* (ABBA), *Suck My Kiss* (The Red Hot Chili Peppers), and *Kiss from a Rose* (Seal).

How and why did lip kissing become such an iconic symbol of romance? Is it part of ancient courtship practices, as Dan Brown intimates in his best-selling novel *The Da Vinci Code*, where he suggests that Jesus and Mary Magdalene kissed on the lips as a sign of their romantic involvement?[3] Unlikely. The story of the romantic kiss starts in the medieval period, as I will claim in this book. It constitutes a fascinating narrative that coincides with the origins and rise of popular culture (or proto-popular culture), as distinct from traditional, religious, or folk culture. But finding evidence for the first kiss is, ironically, very much like a Dan Brown archeological mystery story. There are no photos or trace clues of that first kiss. The only way to hunt down its emergence is to consider the time frame when romantic kissing becomes a theme in poetic and prose texts. And that time frame, as we shall see, is the medieval period.

The forms and functions of kissing are not, of course, limited to courtship and romance. As a greeting sign it has ancient roots. The act of blowing kisses, for example, originated in Mesopotamia as a means to gain the favor of the gods. It is still around today, even though it has lost its divine connotations, having evolved simply into a form of greeting—blowing a kiss with the fingertips in the direction of the intended recipient conveys affection. As recorded by Herodotus, in Persia, a man of equal rank was greeted with a kiss on the lips and one of a slightly lower rank with a kiss on the cheek.[4] Plainly, these kisses did not have romantic meaning; they were greeting rituals, plain and simple. Likewise, in Slavic cultures, kissing between two men on the lips was, and continues to be, part of salutation etiquette. The ancient Romans also kissed to greet each other. An individual's social status dictated what part of the emperor's body he or she was allowed to kiss, from the cheek down to the foot. The lower the part of the body kissed, the lower the rank of the kisser. Early Christians greeted one another with a "kiss of peace" (called the *osculum pacis*), which was believed to carry the soul of the kisser thus connecting him or her spiritually to the other. The *osculum pacis* became a ritualistic part of the Catholic Mass up until the thirteenth century, when the Church substituted it with a "*pax* (peace) board," which the congregation kissed instead of kissing one another. The Protestant Reformation in the sixteenth century eliminated all forms of kissing from religious services, seeing it as a disgusting carnal act. However, in both Catholicism and Protestantism "breath kissing" was allowed to be a part of marriage ceremonies, symbolizing the spiritual union of the bride and groom. Coincidentally, in ancient Celtic love rituals, too, the breath kiss was seen as an exchange of the breath of life and an intrinsic part of courtship.

Kissing has played significant roles in various religious traditions. Kissing a holy book or icon to show reverence and adoration has ancient roots. Moses is portrayed in images as kissing the stone tablets on which the Ten Commandments were written. Catholics kiss the Pope's toe to show reverence and obedience. In the gospels of Matthew and Mark, Judas betrayed Jesus with a kiss, the sign of obedience at the time, distorted into an act of duplicity. Jews kiss the Western wall of the Holy Temple in Jerusalem during prayer; they also kiss the Torah. Eastern Orthodox Christians kiss the icons around a church and the priest's hand during blessings. Hindus kiss the ground of a temple to acknowledge its sacredness and purity.

Research by anthropologists has shown that a significant percentage of humanity actually does not practice kissing rituals of any kind. In cultures across Africa, the Pacific, and the Americas, kissing simply does not exist or, at least, was not known until contact with Europeans and the advent of global communications technologies, which have spread images of the kiss throughout the world. Even though kissing is now tolerated in many of these cultures, to do so in public is still seen as indecent or at least as uncalled for, given that it is an import from the West. In 1990, the *Beijing Workers' Daily* warned its readers that the kissing custom imported to China from the West was a "vulgar practice" that was suggestive of "cannibalism."[5] Similar reactions can be found in other areas of the world. Anthropologist Leonore Tiefer comments on this situation as follows:

> Sexual kissing is unknown in many societies, including the Balinese, Chamorro, Manus, and Tinguian of Oceania; the Chewa and Thonga of Africa; the Siriono of South America; and the Lepcha of Eurasia. In such cultures, the mouth-to-mouth kiss is considered dangerous, unhealthy, or disgusting, the way Westerners might regard a custom of sticking one's tongue into a lover's nose. When the Thonga first saw Europeans kissing, they laughed, remarking, "Look at them— they eat each other's saliva and dirt."[6]

Osculation in the Ancient World

Lip kissing is known technically as *osculation*. Osculation is not part of the courtship traditions of China or Japan, although it has now spread to those societies as well, thanks, as mentioned, to the influence of the images spread by the mass media and the Internet. In Inuit and Laplander societies romantic partners are more inclined to rub noses than to kiss—a practice found in other parts of the world. Early explorers of the Arctic dubbed this act "the Eskimo kiss." Obviously, what is normal romantic behavior in one system of courtship practices is seen as bizarre or vulgar in another. Lip kissing is indeed a bizarre act, given that it involves an unhygienic exchange of saliva, as the young Stephen Dedalus intimated in James Joyce's *Portrait of the Artist as a Young Man,* "Why do people do that with their faces?"[7]

The scientific study of kissing is known as *philematology.* According to some scientists, osculation may have ancient roots, appearing in India as far back as the 1500s BCE. The Vedic writings of that period mention lovers "sniffing" each other with their mouths and "smelling each other." As philematologist Sheril Kirshenbaum writes: "In the Vedic texts no word exists for 'kiss,' but the same word is employed to mean both 'sniff' and 'smell,' and also has connotations of touch."[8] From there, osculation is believed to have been exported westward by Alexander the Great after conquering the Punjab in 326 BCE.[9] Representations of osculation have also been found on two thousand year-old Peruvian pots and vases and in various tribal African societies, as anthropologist Nicholas Perella writes.[10] But did the lip kiss of these ancient cultures have the meaning that it does today, namely as a symbol of romantic love? The fact that a word for *kiss* did not exist, as Kirshenbaum points out, is strong indirect evidence that there was no consciousness of kissing as a romantic act. Subsequent Indian texts, moreover, suggest that osculation had a purely erogenous function from the outset. The fourth century BCE epic poem, the *Mahabharata,* describes lovers as salaciously setting "mouth to mouth" or "drinking the moisture of the lips."[11] In the *Kama Sutra,* an early treatise on sexual techniques put together around the third century CE, osculation is, in fact, described as part of sexual fun and games. Kirshenbaum describes the relevant part of the text as follows:

> An entire chapter is devoted to the topic of kissing a lover, with instructions on when and where to kiss the body, including the forehead, the eyes, the cheeks, the throat, the bosom, the

breasts, the lips, and the interior of the mouth. The text goes on to describe four methods of kissing—moderate, contracted, pressed, and soft—and lays out three kinds of kisses by a young girl or virgin: nominal kiss (the girl touches lips with her lover but does not herself do anything), throbbing kiss (the girl, setting aside her bashfulness a little, responds with her lower but not upper lip), touching kiss (the girl touches her lover's lips with her tongue, closes her eyes, and lays her hands on her lover's hands).[12]

These texts are highly suggestive that lip kissing was indeed an ancient practice, but that it was part of sex, given that the lips are sensitive erogenous organs. The same or parallel sexual portrayals of the kiss can be gleaned from other ancient works, such as the comedies of Aristophanes, where kissing and sex are connected constantly. As the greatest ancient Greek writer of comedy, Aristophanes's plays are imbued with a rollicking wit, aiming to criticize social mores and political hypocrisy. The kissing that goes on in his plays is prurient, not romantic. Osculation also appears in ancient Egyptian art. But in this case, archeologists conjecture that it may have represented "giving or exchanging life," in the same way that the *osculum pacis* did in later Western culture. The Romans also kissed passionately on the lips—an act they called *savium*. They contrasted this with *osculum* and *basium*, which meant respectively a "friendship kiss" and a "love kiss." Roman couples would actually announce their marriage intentions by kissing mouth-to-mouth in front of their families. It was, thus, a kind of announcement gesture—informing everyone that the couple intended to be united physically. Of all the ancient practices involving osculation, this is probably the one that seems to come closest to the meaning of kissing as a romantic act.

The Romans also passed an unusual law punishing anyone caught perpetrating unwanted kisses among citizens of equal social standing. The Roman emperor Tiberius even issued a decree banning lip kissing, because he believed it was responsible for the spread of an unpleasant fungoid disease that disfigured the faces and bodies of Roman nobles.[13] But, if lip kissing was so widespread, why did it not survive as a courtship or romantic gesture in any of these societies until its emergence (or reemergence) in the medieval period, as will be discussed? Interpreting ancient practices in modern terms is fraught with too many dangers of misconception. Indeed, tracing the origins of romantic kissing to the ancient world is an inferential process at best, a kind of "retrofitting" process at worst (i.e., an unconscious attempt to fit or impose contemporary views of the act onto the past). It may seem like an overly exacting point, but there is a difference between kissing the body, including the lips, for sexual excitement and kissing someone on the lips for romantic reasons.

In the Bible, one can find many descriptions of lip kissing, especially among people having affairs beyond their marriages. In the Second Book of Samuel there is the story of a woman tempting a man by kissing him: "With her flattering lips she forced him." In the Song of Songs (or of Solomon) we come across passages such as, "Let him kiss me with the kisses of his mouth: for thy love is better than wine" (1:2). These seem to suggest that osculation was indeed a romantic act. Biblical scholarship prefers, traditionally, to see in the poem a metaphor for divine love, not romantic love. Some modern commentators see it as essentially a work of erotica. Jennifer Wright Knust, for example, portrays the Song as a paean to unmarried sex.[14] Michael Coogan argues that the entire Bible, much like many other ancient texts, is really a treatise on sexual relations.[15] Despite such suggestive passages there is no hermeneutic evidence to indicate that the lip kissing described in them prefigures the romantic kiss as we know it today.

The problem is that we tend to interpret the Bible in a retrofitting way, that is, as describing the same practices as our modern-day ones. That is what Dan Brown did in *The Da Vinci Code*.[16] The hero, a Harvard professor named Robert Langdon, attempts to solve an intriguing historical mystery connecting Jesus and Mary Magdalene by using his knowledge of "symbology" (a misnomer for semiotics). A part of the allure of that novel is due, needless to say, to its intricate mystery plot. But a larger part is due to the ways in which Brown portrays Mary Magdalene as a symbol of the victimization endured by women living in patriarchal societies. The Code, when cracked, reveals that Mary Magdalene was the wife of Jesus and carried his baby (the Holy Grail), surviving evil forces within the Church that have attempted throughout the ages to suppress this fact. All through the novel Brown makes reference to "scholarly research" suggesting that Mary and Jesus kissed each other romantically on the lips. But there is no such research, just baseless and spurious conjectures by self-appointed conspiracy theorists. The novel's enormous success was a result of Brown's cleverness in tapping into a growing desire in the contemporary world to restore women to their original roles as leaders of Christianity. But did Mary and Jesus really kiss on the lips? Even in the Gnostic Gospel of Philip, which mentions the couple kissing, the part that would tell us where they kissed is missing and thus lost forever. It reads as follows:

> The companion of the . . . is Mary of Magdala. The . . . her more than . . . the disciples, . . . kissed her often on her . . . [17]

Other ancient texts contain allusions to lip kissing as part of lovemaking. For example, the Greek historian Plutarch wrote, in his *Parallel Lives,* that Cleopatra dreamt about her first kiss with Mark Antony, seemingly planning her seduction carefully and methodically with it. Was Plutarch using literary license? Did the ill-fated couple truly embrace in romantic osculation? Again, there is no other textual evidence to suggest that they did.

Perhaps the most suggestive of all ancient writing in this regard is the love poetry of the first-century Roman writer Catullus, who extols the lip kiss as a passionate and erotic act.[18]

His best-known poems tell of his love for an aristocratic Roman woman called Lesbia. In Song 5 of *To Lesbia*, he writes:

> Give me a thousand kisses
> a hundred more, another thousand, and another hundred,
> and, when we've counted up the many thousands,
> confuse them so as not to know them all,
> so that no enemy may cast an evil eye,
> by knowing that there were so many kisses.[19]

Significantly, the kissing in the poem takes place after the setting of the sun—a typical allusion to death—and is portrayed as a magical force that offers protection against the evil eye. Thus, there is much more going on in Catullus's poem metaphorically than a straightforward description of romantic osculation. Nevertheless, there is a possibility that his poetry had, overall, a latent effect on the unconscious interpretation of lip kissing as a romantic act, lying dormant (so to speak) for centuries, and surfacing to awareness in the medieval period. But, then, most people in that era would not have been familiar with Catullus or the poetry of Lucretius, another famous Roman poet, which also refers to kissing as a passionate act:

> They grip, they squeeze, their humid tongues they dart,
> As each would force their way t'other's heart.[20]

Lucretius seems to be describing what we could call today a French kiss. And, more significantly, he appears to portray the kiss as the opening tactic in capturing the heart. The poem in which this passage appears, *De rerum natura* (*On the Nature of Things*) is not, actually, a love poem. It is a philosophical and scientific poem that Lucretius wrote in order to free humanity from religious superstition and the fear of death. He was inspired by the writings of the Greek philosopher Epicurus, and the poem reflects the Epicurean ideals of a tranquil mind and freedom from irrational fear. This fact makes the interpretation of these lines even more difficult.

Aware of the power of the kiss, yet another Roman poet, Ovid, advises male suitors in his *Ars amatoria* ("The Art of Love") to use the kiss as an opening tactic as follows:

> Kiss, if you can: resistance if she make,
> And will not give you kisses, let her take.
> Fie, fie, you naughty man, and of course;
> She struggles but to be subdued by force.[21]

Ovid's poetic warning to men is hard to interpret from the modern perspective. Is he telling men that they should take sexual advantage of women with the kiss? Is he indirectly portraying a kind of indirect popular psychology of male sexuality? Again, it is hard, if not impossible to pin down the meaning of a passage such as this one. The *Ars amatoria* is a kind of manual in verse on how to find and keep a lover. Two of its three books are addressed to men and one to women. They are all written in a humorous, satirical style. So, it is likely that he is making fun of masculine lovemaking, not endorsing it.

Overall, it is nearly impossible to infer anything substantive from the ancient texts with regard to romantic kissing. We have to conjecture that either the romantic kiss, as we know it, appears at different times and in different parts of the world in parallel ways, or else that what the texts described was something different. If lip kissing in the ancient world was indeed part of romance, as Kirshenbaum believes, one would then have to explain its disappearance from the societies that apparently practiced it as having a cultural source: "Mouth-to-mouth kissing may have been present and later disappeared among some cultures for social reasons, such as the discouragement of women's sexuality."[22] This may be true, but it is impossible to find real evidence to substantiate this conjecture. We assume that kissing has ancient origins because it has become so widespread, a fact that has unconsciously led us to believe that it is part of the species, not an act originating in a particular culture at a particular point in time. It is estimated, as Kirshenbaum notes, "that over six billion of us from east to west kiss regularly, lip to lip, as a social and romantic custom."[23] This bespeaks more of the power of Western popular culture today, as it spreads throughout the world through technology, than it does of some ancient courtship mechanism present in all humanity. Lip contact requires interpretation. It can be sexual; it can be social; it can be sacred. It can also be romantic. But there is no evidence to suggest that it was interpreted *primarily* in this way before the medieval period.

The Medieval Period

American author James Jones writes the following insightful words in his famous novel, *From Here to Eternity*: "The taboo said you never kissed a whore. They didn't like it. Their kiss was private, like most women's bodies."[24] In a scene in the movie *Pretty Woman*, Julia Roberts, in the role of prostitute Vivian Ward, proclaims that she will have sex with her clients, but not kiss them, because she wants to avoid developing any romantic feelings for them. As these fictional representations suggest, and anthropological research actually shows, prostitutes refrain from kissing their clients to avoid feelings of romance. As Kirshenbaum puts it:

> Both prostitutes and their clients instinctively seem to sense there is more to a kiss than to other sexual acts—that it's in a different category. And, indeed, in social surveys, people rate kissing as more intimate than almost every other kind of activity. It also garners more attention in serious relationships than in casual sexual encounters, and scientists are discovering some fascinating reasons why. The warm fuzzy feelings that we attach to kissing probably have a lot to do with the hormones coursing through our bodies as a result.[25]

The origins of this deeply engrained perception of the kiss as something more than a prelude to sex, or as something that goes beyond sex, can be traced back to the medieval period. In the Catholic medieval marriage ceremony, the *osculum pacis* was a central ritual. It was performed as an exchange of breath through the mouth, indicating both a sign of peace and an exchange of souls. It was also performed as a cheek kiss in some versions of the ceremony. Actual lip touching was frowned upon, since it had sexual implications. At a certain point in time (around the late eleventh and early twelfth centuries), the lip kiss started surfacing in stories, legends, and other forms of popular writing. Osculation had made an entrance onto the cultural stage as something that was both subversive of the cultural order and symbolic of unfettered (unarranged) romance. To marry outside of family-approved unions was considered morally wrong. In the early popular writings the lip kiss was portrayed as going against such moral restrictions and as an act of true love, in contrast to forced (planned) love. Secret lovers kissed and embraced passionately in both poetry and prose. The subtext was transparent: "I love this man or woman, no matter what my family or society thinks!" From there, it was a very short step to enshrining the act into a sui generis (unofficial) romantic courtship gesture into groupthink. A new poetic tradition, called "courtly love," emerged. It was hugely popular, centering on the power of the kiss to make people fall in love with each other. Significantly, the language of the poetry was that of common people (the emerging Romance tongues), not Latin. The seeds for the rise of popular culture had been sown. The unspoken rules of this new form of lovemaking were associated with a new code of chivalry. According to the traditional code, a true knight had to show devotion to the church and his country and treat women with great respect. The new freedom to express love freely and openly turned everyone into a knight. The *De amore* (*The Art of Courtly Love*), written in 1185 by Andreas Capellanus, lists a whole set of principles of this new chivalric code, such as the following: "Marriage is no real excuse for not loving," "He who is not jealous cannot love," "No one can be bound by a double love."[26]

    With the rise of courtly love writing and, a little later, with the emergence of the *Commedia dell'Arte,* which satirized romantic love, one can make a strong case that the public enactment of romance had become a widespread practice. The *Commedia* was a popular form of comedy, performed by professional actors who worked on simple platforms in market squares. Many of its comedic routines satirized romance, as well as the pretensions of religious traditions. The two most prevalent forms of popular culture to this day—romantic stories and romantic satire—had arrived, appealing to large groups of people. They revealed "what the people make, or do, for themselves," as O'Brien and Szeman characterize the ontological fabric of this form of culture.[27]

The identity of the actual couple who performed the first kiss is, of course, unknown. However, the chivalric literature of the era gave the first couple a name, Romeo and Juliet, whoever they represented in real life. It was Shakespeare who made that couple famous, but their love story comes out of medieval lore, representing a narrative plea for freedom of choice in matters of love. The kiss between Romeo and Juliet became so powerful as a symbol of liberation that it has since been depicted in drama, narratives, poetry, art, and other artistic media as something unique in the history of civilization.

Shakespeare probably got his story from a 1562 narrative poem by Arthur Brooke, *The Tragical History of Romeo and Juliet*. Brooke's poem was a translation and adaptation of *Giulietta e Romeo* by the Italian writer Matteo Bandello in 1554. The earliest written version of the tale dates back to a 1476 story, written by Masuccio Salernitano, who inserted it in his collection called *Il Novellino*.[28] But the proto-story of two lovers who go against the wishes of their families is older still, going back to the early medieval period. Romeo and Juliet were fictional metaphors of star-crossed lovers who dared to defy the social status quo in order to be true to their hearts. It is in the fateful Act V of Shakespeare's play that the meaning of kissing as a profound act of love and rebellion at once becomes palpable. Heartbroken upon hearing of Juliet's death, which unbeknownst to Romeo was faked by Juliet, he drinks poison in front of Juliet's "corpse," kissing her and uttering the words: "Thus with a kiss I die."[29]

There is some speculation that the Romeo and Juliet saga may have been modeled on the story of two historical personages—the twelfth-century philosopher Peter Abelard and his paramour Héloïse. Their story certainly had all the ingredients of a legendary tale of ill-fated romance. Abelard began tutoring Héloïse, the niece of a canon of the Cathedral of Notre-Dame in Paris, in 1117. They fell in love and secretly married after Héloïse gave birth to a son. Abelard then persuaded Héloïse to take holy vows. Her uncle, convinced that Abelard had abandoned Héloïse, had him castrated. Abelard later founded a chapel and oratory called the Paraclete, where Héloïse became abbess. In 1125 he became abbot of the monastery at Saint-Gildas-de-Rhuis. About 1132 the two lovers began their famous correspondence, which contains some of the most moving love passages ever written. Upon his death, Abelard's body was taken to the Paraclete; and when Héloïse died she was buried beside him. Their bodies now lie in a single tomb in the Père Lachaise cemetery in Paris. Their story was known throughout medieval society. Were they the original Romeo and Juliet couple? In his autobiography, *The Story of My Misfortunes*, Abelard indicates that he dreamt of kissing Héloïse long before he got the opportunity to do so.[30] The kiss that Abelard dreamt about would certainly have flown in the face of all canons of decency of the era. It would have constituted a sign of rebellion and true passion at once.

Romantic kissing spread quickly throughout Europe and subsequently to other parts of the world, as the postmedieval writings of various nations indicate. Russia was probably the first society to incorporate the lip kiss into its marriage ceremonies. Some of the new practices appear strange and even weird to us today. In Italy, a law was passed stating that if the bride or the groom died before the kiss on the wedding day, every wedding gift had to be given back. In sixteenth-century England, an apple was prepared by piercing it with as many cloves as the fruit could hold. A lass then carried the apple with her to the fair looking for a lad she thought worth kissing. To such a lad she would then offer the apple, and once he had selected and chewed one of the cloves, they would share a kiss. After that, he would take possession of the apple and venture off in search of another lass with whom to continue the game. Practices centered on the kiss started proliferating throughout Europe.[31] So too did philosophical and scientific treatises on lip kissing. In the seventeenth century, a scholar named Martin von Kempe compiled a thousand-page encyclopedia of kissing practices that recognized 20 different varieties.[32] In his *Art of Courtly Love*, Capellanus depicts the lip kiss as an expression of "pure love." The Renaissance philosopher Giovanni Pico della Mirandola also writes about the importance of lovers exchanging kisses in his *Commentary on a Love Song of Girolamo Benivieni*, written in 1486, as follows: "Pouring out their souls one into the other with kisses, they will not exchange their souls so much as perfectly unite together, so that each of them may be said to be two souls and both of them one soul only."[33] This quote recalls the derivation of the romantic kiss from the *osculum pacis*, extending it literally to the contact of the lips. As we read in the sixteenth-century *Perfumed Garden*, written by a Tunisian sheik called Umar Ibn Muhammad el-Nefzawi, the romantic kiss had spread to other parts of the world. In it, the sheik writes: "The kiss on the mouth, on the two cheeks, upon the neck are gifts of God."[34]

Anthropologist Nicholas Perella also traces the origins of romantic lip kissing to the medieval period, calling it the "soul-in-the-kiss conceit."[35] So too does Willem Frijhoff, who explains its origins as follows:

> In the fairy-tale of the Sleeping Beauty, kissed back to life by a foreign prince, this motive finds its supreme expression. Linked with Christian themes, this kiss conceit—with its powerful background of sacred practice—develops into several amatory conceits of a more profane nature: in the Middle Ages, the kiss is mainly a kiss of love, but love at the same time means living.[36]

There is no denying that osculation does produce the physical and psychological reactions that are associated with sexual desire. But it is from the chivalric love code of the medieval period that we have inherited our interpretation of that act as something separate from sexual love, or more accurately, as indicating something more than just sex. This code was especially liberating for women, who were expected to be subservient to men and their families as housewives and mothers. As an overt sign of this liberation, the kiss had estrogen imprinted deeply in it. Kirshenbaum makes a strong case that kissing has always constituted a means for women to decide whether to pursue a deeper connection with a potential partner—women kiss to feel the partner out, emotionally and even sexually, whereas men tend to describe the kiss as a means to an end (sex). This topic will be discussed further in the final chapter. Suffice it to say here that the etiology of this differential physical response is not a genetic endowment; we have inherited it from the unconscious forces of historical transmission.

Because the kiss originated as a need to subvert the extant religious and patriarchal order in medieval Europe, it acquired great appeal wherever it was introduced through narratives, poetry, and visual art. In the modern world, entire sectors of popular culture are devoted to the art of kissing, from Harlequin romances to websites that give advice on how to kiss someone effectively. Most of the remainder of this book will deal with the entrenchment of the kiss in popular culture—a culture based on the body, not on its denial.

Theorizing the Kiss

Surfacing in medieval poetry and narratives, the kiss has captured the popular imagination ever since. It has actually changed our biology. Scientists have shown that the act of kissing signals our brains to produce oxytocin, a hormone that triggers pleasurable and erotic feelings. To use the language of a romance writer, a kiss engages every fiber of our being, turning over our stomach and sending goose bumps up our spine. A kiss unites the physical, sexual part of lovemaking with the romantic, spiritual part, imbuing courtship with great meaning. The role of oxytocin in this process is explained by Kirshenbaum as follows:

> Often called the "love hormone," oxytocin is inextricably involved in intimacy, and has been shown to have extremely powerful effects in a laboratory setting. For example, when it is injected into the brain of a virgin female rat, this hormone causes her to immediately adopt the babies of another rat as her own. No one has tried the above experiment in women (for reasons that are perhaps obvious), but we know oxytocin works similarly in our own species. It is responsible for cementing the connection between parent and child and also serves to trigger lactation in new mothers. It helps to regulate mood and acts as a natural painkiller.[37]

Scientists have put forward a host of theories about the biological and evolutionary roots of the kiss. They are worth going over here. Some argue that the source of osculation lies in the need to transfer sebum, the substance that lubricates our skin and hair, so that mating partners can achieve a form of chemical bonding. Others believe that we kiss because the lips, tongue, and interior of the mouth are highly sensitive erogenous zones connected to the limbic system, the oldest part of the brain and the source of sexual pleasure.[38] The lips have nerve endings that are highly sensitive to incoming stimuli, from pressure to temperature. Just a light touch on the lips will stimulate them sexually, given the right atmosphere and a willingness to engage in romance.

There is also a theory that kissing might be connected to the tendency of mothers to premasticate food for their offspring, that is, to chew their food and pass it on to their babies, mouth-to-mouth.[39] This makes some sense, since it posits that osculation derives from an action that ensured survival, encoded over time into cultural practices and symbolism. But then how could an act born of the love felt by a mother chewing food for her baby evolve into an act of pure romance? Supporters of the theory claim that a form of chewing between lovers was once practiced in the Ziller Valley of central Europe.[40] The exchange of premasticated substances between a male and a female was part of courtship. If a female accepted the wad, it meant she returned her partner's love. For psychoanalyst Sigmund Freud, too, kissing was a "relic gesture," a subconscious return to suckling at the mother's breast.[41] Suckling is not just pleasurable, but also sexual. This is why Freud claimed that sucking the thumb in childhood replaced breast suckling, emerging after the infant had been weaned from the breast. Since this was not as pleasurable as breast suckling, at adolescence, the child would proceed to find the lips of another person to replace the mother's breast.[42] As Adrianne Blue has remarked, for Freud kissing "tells the whole story of humankind."[43] But, other than Freud's interesting speculative views themselves, there is no scientific evidence to link kissing with suckling. They just look similar.

In other attempts to theorize the origins of osculation, it is viewed as a biological "lie-detection system." It is explained as an act allowing prospective mates to taste and smell each other out for compatibility. In this view, humans are said to judge potential mates on the quality of their kiss as a sign of a potential lover's personality and willingness to commit. It is not unlike what snails do when they appear to caress each other with their antennae, or what birds do when they touch beaks, or what bonobos do when they seem to engage in full-fledged tongue-on-tongue kissing. In the latter case, actually, ethologists have found that it is done to reduce the tension after a dispute, constituting more a gesture of reconciliation, than a sign of romance. In her classic book, *In the Shadow of Man*, primatologist Jane Goodall writes: "I saw one female, newly arrived in a group, hurry up to a big male and hold her hand toward him. Almost regally he reached out, clasped her hand in his, drew it toward him, and kissed it with his lips."[44] Whatever the interpretation of animal kissing may be, it is certainly far from being analogous to what humans do when they kiss romantically. Darwin, too, talked about chimpanzees kissing and hugging.[45] But does such behavior carry within it the meaning of romance, in the human sense? Maybe it is more a form of smelling or sexual sniffing. Incidentally, in his interesting book, *Adam's Navel*, Michael Sims believes that kissing and smelling in romance may have had a common origin, a fact that is supported somewhat by the coincidence that words for "kiss" and "smell" are the same in many modern-day tribes.[46]

Anthropologist Desmond Morris traces the origins of kissing to what he calls a "genital echo."[47] He maintains that it mirrors genital contact, given that the lips recall the labia by virtue of their physical resemblance to them. As such, it is a part of sexual courtship involving mental images of the female's sexuality that are translated in the form of lip actions and movements. Certainly, female lips are erotic, an intuitive fact that the cosmetics industry certainly understands via advertising. Interestingly, and suggestively, research points to the tendency of men as being attracted to women with naturally large lips, which seem to signal arousal and openness.[48] Morris's theory is also consistent with a neuroscientific theory that mirror neurons exist in the brain, firing messages in response to someone else's experiences, as if they were happening to us. This might explain why, unconsciously, we interpret lips as genitalia; or maybe not. The verdict on the presence of mirror neurons is still out.

The emergence of so many theories trying to explain the evolutionary origins and significance of kissing divulges, actually, that we cannot make up their minds about it. As Kirshenbaum notes, the debate goes back to Darwin, and the confusion over "kissing-like-behaviors," which is a much broader category of sexual behavior than is the romantic kiss.[49] It is a leap of scientific faith to assert that kissing is hardwired in the brain by biology. If it is so wired within us, why is it unknown to so many people in the world, or at least was before the advent of the global village? To cite Kirshenbaum again, the early kissing behaviors may have been nothing more that greeting gestures, a fact borne out by the continued use of kissing to this day as a greeting or identification protocol:

> Many early cultures became accustomed to what's called the "oceanic kiss," so named to describe a traditional greeting in Polynesia. Such a "kiss" involves going back and forth across the nose to smell another person for the purpose of identification, and probably served as a reliable means to recognize and reconnect with relatives and friends, and perhaps even provide clues about a person's health. [50]

The application of the word *kiss* to animal behaviors is a human decision—a decision that parallels our use of the word *dance* to describe the movements of honeybees indicating the presence of a food source to other members of the hive. The behaviors of dogs, seals, chimps, gulls, and many birds are all perceived by us to be very similar to our kisses and thus we label them in this way. But these tags are analogies, no more, no less. Using these words, however, influences us conceptually into seeing the human meanings encoded by those words in the animal activities. This was the caveat issued by the great Estonian biologist Jakob von Uexküll.[51] Uexküll observed that each animal has an inner world that processes the same information of the outside world available to everyone selectively and in a species-specific way. There is no way to understand what a nonhuman animal does with that information by observing the behaviors it triggers, since these are part of the animal's biological heritage, not ours. In a similar fashion, Kirshenbaum writes as follows:

> Behavioral scientists find it extremely difficult to describe the emotional lives of animals other than themselves. Because different species may process information and interpret the world in vastly different ways, it's not possible for a human to "know" what another animal is feeling and thinking in any meaningful sense of the term.

Whatever its biological origins, the romantic kiss affects people deeply. The body reacts as a total entity to the act, literally from head to toe. When the kiss is first performed by a couple who are attracted strongly to each other, the adrenalin and blood rush is unmistakable. Over time that rush will diminish and the kiss will evolve into an act of affection and a promise of faithfulness. But its "fire" can easily be reignited under various circumstances. Kissing involves muscles working together, the most important of which being the *orbicularis oris*, known as the "kissing muscle," which is a round band of muscle encircling the lips, extending to the chin and running between the nose and upper lip. Special sebaceous glands at the edges of the lips and inside the mouth, which develop at puberty, release chemical reactions that stimulate sexual desire. Adrenalin, serotonin, dopamine, and oxytocin are activated in the act, to varying degrees, along with the natural endorphins. All these produce euphoria or ecstasy. Heartbeat increases and blood vessels dilate during kissing, so that the body receives more oxygen than normal. To quote Michael Sims, when we kiss the relevant sexual parts of the body "are networked like computer systems to facilitate communication between each other."[52]

Lip contact also unleashes cortisol, which is associated with stress. Researchers have found that both sexes experience a decline in cortisol after kissing, a sign that stress levels are lowered. All this is reported in a recent book by biological anthropologist, Helen Fisher, called *Why Him? Why Her?* in which she argues that men and women kiss to assess genetic compatibility, attributing this to the reason why kissing can create so-called sparks.[53] We also determine compatibility via the sense of smell, but saliva exchange may be a genetic compatibility-marker as well, especially since there is testosterone in saliva and this might unconsciously trigger estrogen in women's saliva, with men assessing the level of estrogen (again unconsciously) to determine her state of fertility. In women, kissing releases dopamine, which fosters feelings of love and sexual intimacy. They also tend to see kissing behavior as a gauge of how their amorous relationship is progressing. But arousal, mate-assessment, and other such functions can be obtained in many other ways than kissing. As Albert Einstein once put it, "How on earth are you ever going to explain in terms of chemistry and physics so important a biological phenomenon as first love?"[54] The emergence of the romantic kiss is certainly connected to our biology, but in larger part it is connected to history and our need to change it through acts and symbols of rebellion and of deeper meanings. As Kirshenbaum emphasizes, the kiss has evolved into a unique gesture that symbolizes the power of love perfectly:

> When it comes to matters of the heart, the kiss has evolved to foster feelings of connection, romance, and intimacy—feelings that, when the match is right, may be promoted indefinitely between individuals. It can be scientifically investigated, studied, and even dissected from every angle, but in the end we're left with one real and firm conclusion. Kissing is a type of universal language, best interpreted by those involved in the exchange.[55]

The Subversive Power of the Kiss

Maybe the conditions for the performance of the first lip kiss were pre-wired in the brain by evolution. But that kiss has certainly become much more than an act of sexual desire connected with evolutionary processes. As discussed above, and as will be elaborated throughout this book, it was an act of defiance, encouraging the rise of a culture of free expression—free from the yoke of familial and religious traditions where marriages were arranged by others, not by the lovers themselves. As such, it had subversive power, not just romantic and sexual power, evolving into a perfect symbol of free romance in the popular imagination. This is why the history of the kiss has much more to do with cultural change than with biological adaptation. A hundred years ago, it was normal to think that women would swoon when kissed by their lovers, as the novels of the time inform us. Today, if fainting or swooning occurred in a movie theater during a kiss, we would see this as bizarre. The Kinsey Institute, which studies human sexuality, describes an individual's response to kissing as a combination of factors, especially one's feelings toward the kisser. If we are kissed by someone we do not like, or against our will, we will hardly get goose bumps from it. It will revolt us.

The proof that the kiss retains its original subversive power can be found anecdotally in the fact that it can occur outside of marriage, providing an opening gambit for escaping a boring situation and for entering into a world of enticement. The extramarital affair starts with a kiss. The stories of how this act leads either to bliss or, more often, tragedy, abound. The troubadours in the Middle Ages -poet-musicians who flourished in southern France in the 1100s and 1200s—were aware of the betrayal power of kissing in this sense. This is why they homogenized the kiss as an act of pure love in their songs, even as they engaged in trysts with women other than their own partners. Here is an example of one of their poems, written by an unknown troubadour:

> Come let us kiss, dear lover, you and I,
> Within the meads where pretty song-birds fly;
> We will do all despite the jealous eye:
> Ah God, ah God, the dawn! It comes how soon.[56]

The popular literature of the medieval period constitutes the corpus of evidence that the expression of free love had emerged as a pattern in everyday life. The troubadours composed poetry in Provençal, or *langue d'oc*. The *canso d'amor* (love song) was their mainstay genre. In the *canso*, the lover imagines the lady of his desires as the model of virtue, and then he dedicates his talents to singing her praises. The troubadours' praise of love stood in direct contrast to traditional Christian morality. Medieval epic poems were also popular. Called *chansons de geste*, these were performed in public places by *jongleurs* to musical accompaniment. The most famous was *The Song of*

Roland (about 1100). It describes an incident during a campaign led by Charlemagne. He was returning from an expedition there in 778 when a mountain people called the Basques ambushed and wiped out his army. At about the same time, the *romance* became highly popular. Romances told of knightly deeds and chivalry. They were long fictional works, often filled with fantastic adventures. One of the greatest romances of the era is the *Romance of the Rose*, written by Guillaume de Lorris in the early 1200s as an allegory about love.[57] Jean de Meun continued the poem from about 1275 to 1280 as a satire on the society of his time. Perhaps the best-known medieval romance was *Sir Gawain and the Green Knight*, written by an unknown English author in the late 1300s. Gawain was a knight and nephew of the legendary King Arthur of medieval Britain. He died fighting his treacherous kinsman Modred in the chronicle tradition of Arthurian narratives that developed from Geoffrey of Monmouth's *History of the Kings of Britain* (about 1136). In medieval French and German accounts, Gawain is portrayed as both the finest model of chivalry and a prime example of hypocrisy. This confusion over his character as both a hero and a villain is due no doubt to his amorous exploits, which include exchanging seductive kisses with a married lady of his desires.

The origin of the kiss in medieval popular culture tells a substory of empowerment and liberation.[58] Perhaps those who introduced kissing into the realm of the popular, got their cue from a pagan myth that was certainly well-known at the time—the myth of Psyche and Cupid. Psyche was a young beautiful woman who loved, and was loved by, Cupid. In sculptures they are portrayed as embraced in a kissing posture that was commonly interpreted as an act that united them spiritually, thus bridging the spiritual and the physical. Psyche (which means *soul* in Greek) is the crucial character. She represents the human soul's encounter with love and passion (Cupid) and its struggle to achieve liberation from earthly limitations. Psyche was liberated by Cupid to become a powerful goddess.

Was it his kiss that did it? The analogy to the liberating force of the kiss for medieval womanhood is unmistakable. Since then, courtship decisions have gradually moved away from someone else imposing them on women, to women making them for themselves.

CHAPTER 2

The Kiss in Symbol, Ritual, and Myth

Rose is a rose is a rose.
—Gertrude Stein (1874–1946)

What motivates human beings to do the things they do? From ancient philosophy to modern-day psychology and sociobiology, no satisfactory answer to this question has ever emerged. A more manageable version of this question would be: What is the meaning of the things that human beings produce? That is the core query that guides the discipline of semiotics—the science of meaning. As a general framework of ontological inquiry, semiotic method suggests that to understand something enigmatic like the kiss, it is necessary to study it as a *sign*, that is, as something that stands for a range of meanings that connect it to other meaning structures in the network of signs that the Estonian semiotician, Yuri Lotman, called the *semiosphere*—the universe of signs in which the human mind is immersed.[1]

The kiss is much more than an instinctual response to sexual signals. Since the medieval period it has become a sign of romantic love connected to particular rituals and symbolism throughout the world. Roses and chocolate, for example, are cultural offshoots of the kiss that derive metaphorically from its imagined sweet taste and smell.[2] This became clear early on, as evidenced by a French custom of the medieval era. As the moon went through all its phases a romantic couple was supposed to drink a brew called metheglin, which was made from honey, because it was supposed to enhance their feelings of attachment. From this we eventually developed the notion of the *honeymoon*, or the belief that a period of romance after marriage was critical for the newlyweds to strengthen the love knot that they had just tied, in a metaphorical saccharine way. Actually, the original idea of a post-wedding period comes from ancient Babylonia when newlyweds were expected to be alone for a period of a month, so that they could get a head start on procreation. But the idea of a "sweet" or "honey" period under the "moon" for couples to enact their romance starts in the medieval period. Since then the gustatory link between a sweet substance such as chocolate and romance was forged indelibly. Interestingly, an Italian candy manufacturer (Perugina) has become famous for its *Baci* products (meaning "kisses"). Inside each individually wrapped chocolate a little poem or proverb related to love and romance can be found. The topic of chocolate, roses, and other symbols and rituals connected to romance constitutes a starting point for understanding the connections of the kiss to the rise of popular customs connected with love. The study of such connections is the essence of semiotic method.

Love Symbols

Chocolate was brought to Europe from the New World by the Spaniards, who learned about it from the Aztecs and the Maya, around 1519. It was imported to England about 1657. In the United States, chocolate was first manufactured at Milton Lower Mills, near Dorchester, Massachusetts, in 1765.[3] Since then, it has become one of the more recognized symbols of love in the modern world. On Valentine's Day, for instance, giving a box of chocolates along with flowers and an appropriate card has become a global love ritual.[4] Although we now associate it with sweetness, the word *chocolate* comes from an indigenous word meaning "bitter water." This is likely due to the fact that the fruit of the cacao tree, from which it is made, is bitter. It acquires its sweetness through fermentation. Maya hieroglyphs suggest that it was used for various ceremonial purposes, including as a sexual stimulant, supposedly enhancing the male's prowess in bed and making women more willing to engage in sex. The same view of chocolate surfaced in some parts of Europe among the nobility, after Princess Maria Theresa apparently gave cocoa beans as an engagement gift to Louis XIV. Soon after, chocolate became the rage in France as an aphrodisiac, after sugar was added to it—hence the crystallization of the concept of love as a sweet-tasting experience.[5] None other than the legendary seventeenth-century Italian libertine Giacomo Casanova believed that sweetened chocolate stimulated romantic feelings and augmented male potency. It became a staple of Valentine's Day practices in the twentieth century when chocolate manufacturers started to promote their product as a love stimulant through advertising.[6]

There are several versions to the Valentine's Day story. One goes back to the ancient Romans, who celebrated the fertility feast of Lupercalia on February 15 near the Lupercal, a cave in the Palatine Hill, where, according to Roman mythology, a wolf nursed the infant twins Romulus and Remus, the legendary founders of Rome. During this celebration, the young men struck young women with strips of wolf hide in the belief that the women who took the blows would become more fertile. After the Romans began their conquest of Britain in 43 BCE, the British took over many Roman customs and festivals. One of these was Lupercalia, reshaping it into a Christian one. The association of fertility with wolves seems to reverberate with archetypal overtones. Wolves howl at night, the time of day when they send out their love calls. The modern-day connection of lovemaking to the nighttime may have its source in this ancient ritual.

Another origin story is associated with a priest named Valentine, who was martyred on February 14 in Rome by Claudius the Goth around 269 CE. A basilica was built in his honor in Rome in 350 CE, and a catacomb containing his remains was found on this location. At the time, the emperor had forbidden young men to marry, because he needed them to give up their lives to the military. Valentine disobeyed the emperor's order and secretly married young couples. He was caught in the act and imprisoned. While in jail, he fell in love with the jailor's blind daughter who miraculously regained her sight through his prayerful intercession and the power of his love. His name became associated with love immediately thereafter.

A third story links Valentine's Day to an old English belief that birds choose their mates on February 14. As Chaucer wrote in *The Parlement of Foules (The Parliament of Fowls)*: "For this was on St. Valentine's Day, When every fowl cometh there to choose his mate."[7] The expression "lovebirds" probably comes from this tradition. The same term is used to describe small parrots that are very fond of their mates, sitting next to them for a long period of time. As applied to humans, the word probably goes back to Chaucer's time, as mentioned, but it appears in print for the first time in Dickens's novel *Bleak House* (1868): "Mr. Guppy, going to the window tumbles into a pair of love-birds."[8]

It is impossible to determine which version is the historically correct one.[9] All that can be said is that the modern celebration of love on Valentine's Day has its own rituals and symbols that derive from the free expression of romantic love, rather than from practices connected with arranged courtship. The giving of chocolate at Valentine's is part of the feeling of "sweet magic" that romance is supposed to evoke. The 2000 movie *Chocolat*, based on the novel of the same name by Joanne Harris, brings this out in a cinematically eloquent way.[10] It tells the story of a young mother who arrives at a repressed French village with her six-year-old daughter. She opens a small *chocolaterie* and the chocolate she sells to people changes their lives. Romance is rekindled in an older couple, an elderly man is encouraged to seek out his secret love, and many other romantic miracles are realized—all because of the magical power of chocolate.

Along with a box of chocolates, no Valentine's Day celebration would be complete without flowers and especially roses. In ancient Rome the rose was a symbol of secrecy. This came from the practice of hanging a rose over the door to a room where a secret meeting was going on. The meeting was said to be sub rosa (under the rose). In other parts of the ancient world the rose symbolized feminine beauty and love. Chloris, the Greek goddess of flowers, was thought to have created the rose by giving life to the lifeless body of a nymph. The rose was also connected to Aphrodite. It was her emblem of beauty taken from the blood of Adonis, her dearly beloved. From this history, it is a small step to understanding that, when the lip kiss started signifying free, but often secret, romance in the medieval period, the rose emerged as a perfect symbol of secret love and feminine beauty—amalgamating the Roman and mythological meanings of the flower into a singular sign. In his clever novel, *The Name of the Rose,* semiotician Umberto Eco brings out this symbolism masterfully, taking place in the late medieval period when radical social and cultural changes were taking shape.[11] The rose in the novel is a sign of defiance against the Church-based moral order, which excluded women from social power and relegated them to an arranged courtship system. The rose was, as Eco correctly implies, a veritable sign of liberation from ecclesiastical hegemony. Indirect evidence for this comes from medieval texts such as the *Roman de la rose*, a French allegorical poem mentioned briefly in the previous chapter, which used the rose as a symbol of female beauty and sexuality, given the genital suggestiveness of its physical form.[12] Simply put, when a medieval gentleman gave a female a rose, he would have been communicating love and admiration for her beauty, at the same time that he was issuing her an invitation to enter into a love tryst with him. The rose was the overall symbol of courtly love practices and their liberating force.

As Marilyn Yalom has observed, the appearance of the courtly love tradition in the twelfth century thrust women's physical pleasure and emotional needs to the fore.[13] Courtly lovers were expected to make great sacrifices to the "gentler sex" and prove their love for them, not just assume it. As such, courtly love was not just about marriage—true love could occur between two people who did not even know each other. Secret love rendezvous, betrayals, and all the kinds of sexual entanglements we take for granted today as part of foible-making were acts that had a defiant social tinge to them. This led to gallantry and the tradition of "falling in love," as opposed to being "put into love" by prearranged matchmaking.

Since the medieval period the rose has become the ultimate symbol of romantic love. Even its different colors suggest a kaleidoscope of romantic feelings, with red dominating, given the color's connection to fertility and femininity—a fact that has not escaped the manufacturers of cosmetic products. With a small research team of students at the University of Toronto in the year 2009, we asked a group of people (20 males and 20 females) to identify the different colors of roses they would either prefer to give to, or receive from, a paramour at Valentine's Day. Most selected red as the primary one. Yellow came in second, probably because of its association to feelings of jealousy and thus, indirectly, to love and potential betrayal. This highly informal and limited study is, however, not inconsistent with general research on the chromatic symbolism of the rose.[14] The preference for red is also compatible with Desmond Morris's genital echo hypothesis (mentioned in the previous chapter), explaining, by association, why red is popular in lipsticks and other cosmetics, having been shown to have a sexual effect on men.[15] As Morris suggests the color red announces a kind of "hidden estrus," that unconsciously stimulates sexual feelings in men. Morris's work in this area is synthesized by Kirshenbaum as follows:

> To test the "genital echo" hypothesis, Morris showed male volunteers photographs of women wearing various lipstick colors and asked them to rate the attractiveness of each. The men consistently chose those featuring the brightest (most

aroused-looking) red lips as most appealing. To quote Morris, "These lipstick manufacturers did not create an enhanced mouth; they created a pair of super labia."[16]

The color red is also connected to blood, and the source of blood is the heart. This might explain why that organ has been perceived and represented as a metaphor for love across time and across many cultures. The ancient Egyptians saw the heart as the seat of love, the place where the love feeling originates. Ancient alchemists, too, believed that the heartbeat was in synchrony with the rhythms of love. In her 1991 book on the senses, Diane Ackerman writes: "Throughout history, people have located love in the heart, probably because of its loud, safe, and comforting beat."[17] In Roman mythology, Cupid's arrow pierces the heart, indicating that we cannot escape the all-consuming power of love when it starts to beat within us. This suggests that when love occurs we are inextricably bound to the other person for life. This bond is symbolized by two love symbols—rings and knots—both of which go back considerably in time. Diamond rings, in particular, have been treasured as part of love rituals since their origin in ancient India, indicating precious and eternal union. The "Diamonds are Forever" motif adopted by De Beers, which started way back in a 1948 ad campaign and continues to be a highly successful one, is designed to tap into this latent symbolism.[18] The diamond ring is a promise of everlasting love.

The Roman poet Plautus, writing in the second century BCE, noted that rings had symbolized love even before his era. Some scholars, in fact, trace the love meaning of the ring back to prehistoric times, when inserting the ring into a finger was likely interpreted as simulating sexual intercourse and, thus, the promise of fertility.[19] Rings at wedding ceremonies were exchanged in ancient Egypt. They were worn by the newlyweds on the third finger of the left hand, because it was believed that the vein in that finger ran directly into the heart. The tradition of exchanging gold rings in marriage comes from 860 CE, when Pope Nicholas I issued a decree making it obligatory for wedding bands to be made of gold. This was meant to ensure that the groom's commitment was financial as well as amorous.

Love knots are made of ribbons and, like diamond rings, are perceived broadly to be symbols of everlasting love, representing union through a series of winding, intertwining loops that, like a Möbius strip, have neither a beginning nor an end. It is difficult to sketch out the origin of the knot symbol. Some scholars trace it to Arab courtship traditions; others to the custom of sailors making knots to communicate love messages to secret paramours.[20] Whatever the case may be, there is little doubt that, like the kiss, the knot suggests an eternal embrace and, thus, a timeless union. The kiss is, in effect, a metaphorical knot, uniting two bodies and two souls through the lips.

As one other symbol connected almost universally with love and kissing, the moon stands out prominently. Early peoples thought the moon was a powerful goddess—a fact represented in many operas of the Romantic period, such as Vincenzo Bellini's *Norma* and Giuseppe Verdi's *Il Trovatore*. The ancient Romans called her Luna and the Greeks Artemis. Worship of the moon was widespread in pagan cultures.[21] In *A Midsummer Night's Dream* (Act 1, Scene 1), Shakespeare compared the moon to "a silver bow new-bent in heaven." Wild things are thought to happen when there is a full moon, and unlike love under the stars, lovemaking in the moonlight almost always conveys sadness, betrayal, or some other "lunatic" state.

Love Rituals

Rituals are enactments of symbolism.[22] People use rituals to express symbolically those ideas about themselves and their rapport to the world that are emotionally meaningful. Many of these have an origin in an intuitive sense for the divine. This was certainly true of love rituals. Most ancient cultures believed that specific gods were assigned the task of getting people to fall in love. Two such love deities were Eros and Cupid. Eros meant "desire" in Greek. He was the deity who came from Chaos ("the yawning void"), representing the primal force of sexual desire. He was born from the union of Aphrodite and Ares. The Roman god Cupid was often shown blindfolded to symbolize love's blindness. Whomever his arrow pierced, as we saw, could not escape falling in love. By and large, arranged marriages based on specific rituals were the norm, a tradition that extended well into the medieval period, when marriages were virtually business transactions between families or else stemming from the desire to forge political alliances.[23]

Because they are communally specific, love rituals may seem strange to outsiders. Take, as an example, the ancient tradition in Nordic countries whereby, when a young girl came of age, she would wear an empty sheath on her belt. If a suitor liked her, he would put a knife in the sheath, which the girl would then wear as a sign of betrothal. This may seem strange to us today, with its apparent phallic symbolism, but it really is not much different than giving a ring to a loved one to acknowledge union. It is the act of giving that counts; not what is given. In seventeenth-century Wales, the gift consisted of ornately carved spoons, known as "lovespoons," which a suitor would make himself to show his affection toward his loved one. At about the same time in England, men often sent a pair of gloves to their paramours as an invitation to courtship. If the woman wore the gloves to church on Sunday it signaled her acceptance of the proposal. All such rituals, in the end, recognize the idea of matrimony as a "tie that binds." In some traditional African cultures, long blades of grass are braided together and used to tie the hands of the groom and bride together to symbolize the union. And delicate twine is used in the Hindu wedding ceremony to bind one of the bride's hands to one of the hands of the groom.

The Quakers, more than any other group, have stood for American Puritanism in its most rigid forms perform a surprising ritual (for them) involving the kiss. When pubescent Quakers get together, their favorite activity is a free-for-all kissing game that often ends in bruising and rug burn. The game dates back to the early 1900s. To play, participants divide themselves into mixed gender pairs with one boy left over to be the "winker." The pairs sit on the floor, with each young male hugging a young female from behind. When the selected male winks at a female, she is expected to scamper across the room to kiss him, while her male partner is supposed to do his best to hold her back. Hilarity ensues. In 2002 the British sect of the society issued a statement discouraging the game at official functions, frowning on it, not because of its sexual subtext, but because of political correctness—children and adults do not get to play, thus making it ageist and against a basic tenet of Quaker philosophy, the tenet of equality.

The Quaker ritual is not unlike the kinds of kissing games played out among teenagers throughout modern society, games that are now part of get-together rituals in youth. Such games have included Truth or Dare, Seven Minutes in Heaven, Spin the Bottle, Post Office, among others. They act as icebreakers at parties. The teen-oriented 1996 movie *Clueless* introduced another kissing game for a while, called Suck and Blow, whereby a group of people are supposed to form a circle and pass a playing card around the circle by blowing and sucking air through their mouths. The main point of the game is that when the card slips from the mouths of partners, the two end up giving each other a furtive kiss. Although such games are not being practiced widely today, for the reason that they come not from historical traditions, but from the media and thus are ephemeral, they nonetheless bring out the fact that lovemaking and ritual are intertwined. Without rituals, the act of lovemaking would be a purely physical, instinctual one. Ritual imbues courtship with meaning beyond the physical—a meaning that is also imprinted in attendant symbols such as the ones discussed here.

At the core of most modern-day rituals and customs is the kiss. There is a story about the 1912 graduation class of Syracuse University that has become a legend at the school. The class apparently left behind a stone bench, hoping to start a tradition connected with romance. In the 1950s, for example, it was believed that if a female student was kissed while sitting on the bench she would enhance her chances of finding the right husband. In the 1970s, the tradition was modified to take the emerging new role of women in society into account. It was believed then that if a woman kissed someone on the bench she would successfully graduate and marry someone. Currently, it is believed that if a man and woman kiss while sitting on the bench they will eventually marry each other. In another story, in Guanajuato, Mexico there is a smooching spot called el Callejón del Beso (The Alley of the Kiss), which, according to local legend, was once the final scene of a fatal love-based event. A young woman and her lover met there to elope, but when the woman's father discovered the plan, he stabbed his daughter in the heart. As she lay dying, her lover kissed her hand for the last time. From this last desperate gesture of romantic love, the alley got its name. Today, it is said that anyone who kisses there will receive seven years of romantic happiness and good luck. Thanks to its romantic history, the alley has become a popular tourist attraction.

The story of the kissing post found in Ellis Island's registry room is another relevant one. The post is a renowned column because it is the place where millions of immigrants first met their family and friends after arriving in the United States. It was named the "kissing post" by customs officials because of the joyful reunions and kisses they witnessed between relatives and loved ones and, of course, the many romantic kisses that were performed between reunited lovers. The kissing post came to symbolize freedom, reunion, a new beginning, and love reunion.

One of the more interesting and well-known kissing traditions is the one in which people are supposed to kiss under a mistletoe plant during Christmas.[24] One theory traces the tradition to a Norse myth. The goddess of the sky, Frigg, had two sons, including Balder, the god of light, whom she adored. To protect him from all harm, she cast a spell on all plants, rendering them unable to hurt him. But she overlooked the mistletoe plant. Loki, a god known for his mischief, tricked another god into killing Balder with a spear made of mistletoe. The gods eventually brought Balder back to life, and Frigg declared that the mistletoe would from then on bring love, rather than death, into the world. People started kissing under the mistletoe shortly thereafter, so the legend goes. Another theory claims that the mistletoe was considered to be an aphrodisiac in ancient times, becoming part of marriage ceremonies, and often being placed under the beds of married couples for good luck in conceiving. When this tradition reached England, it was transformed into the current ritual. Young men would kiss unmarried women standing under the mistletoe, plucking a berry from the mistletoe bush after each kiss. It was considered to be bad luck to continue kissing under the bush when all the berries were gone. The kiss was a kind of unstated pledge of marriage compatibility.

Another legend is connected with the ancient Druids who believed that the oak tree was a sacred plant. They worshipped the mistletoe that grew on it. The Roman writer Pliny explains the legend as follows:

> The Druids, for so they call their wizards, esteem nothing more sacred than the mistletoe and the tree on which it grows, provided only that the tree is an oak. The mistletoe is very rarely to be met with; but when it is found, they gather it with solemn ceremony.[25]

The ritualistic use of cards to express love is also an interesting ancient tradition. Recall the story of St. Valentine from above—the imprisoned priest who fell in love with the jailor's daughter. On the night before his execution, he wrote a letter to the girl, signing it with the line "From Your Valentine." Some historians see in that letter the origin of the Valentine card. Others trace it to Chaucer who wrote the following lines in his *Parlement of Foules:*

For this was on seynt Volantynys day
Whan euery bryd comyth there to chese his make.[26]

In contemporary English, this translates as "For this was on Saint Valentine's Day, when every bird comes there to choose his mate." The entreaty to come "there" was via a card. The *Parlement* is a poem written to honor the first anniversary of the engagement of King Richard II of England to Anne of Bohemia. The assumption is that Chaucer was referring to Valentine's Day, but some literary critics speculate that he may be referring to May 3, the celebration of Valentine of Genoa in the liturgical calendar. As in most cases of philological speculation, it must remain just that—speculation.

The first love card was sent by Charles, the Duke of Orleans, in 1415 when he was in prison in the Tower of London. He sent it to his wife. It is on display today at the British Museum. In 1880s England, an interested gentleman could not simply walk up to a young lady and begin a conversation. Once they had been formally introduced, if the gentleman wished to escort the lady home he would present his card to her. At the end of the evening the lady would look over her options and choose her escort. She would notify the lucky gentleman by giving him her own card requesting that he accompany her home. Almost all courting took place in the woman's home, under the eye of watchful parents or guardians. If the relation progressed, the couple might advance to the front porch. Smitten couples rarely saw each other without the presence of a chaperone, and marriage proposals were frequently written in a formal letter.[27]

Love Myths

Many names given to the act of kissing are connected with mythological or philosophical notions. A *Platonic kiss*, for instance, is given on the cheeks between nonsexual lovers. This term is quite interesting because, strangely, the Greek philosopher Plato did not invent it, and, ironically, it was he who saw sexual desire as the basis for spiritual love. It was the Italian

Renaissance philosopher Marsilio Ficino who coined the term "Platonic love" to denote a love that prepared us for the love of God.[28]

The *neck kiss*, also known as the *Dracula kiss*, is a passionate, sensual kiss on the neck. It is perhaps the kiss that is most associated with a mythic legend that has become an intrinsic part of popular narratives—the vampire myth.

A few years back, *Cosmopolitan* magazine reported that the Dracula kiss was voted the most erotic of all kisses by women, however offering no explanation for this.[29] Obviously, it is connected to the Dracula legend. As we know him, Dracula was introduced to the modern world by Bram Stoker in his eponymous novel of 1897.[30] Coming at the end of the Romantic era, the Dracula figure fit in perfectly with the times, challenging authority, exuding passion and sexual power, and resuscitating the mythic search for immortality. Belief in vampirism may have existed in ancient times, although the evidence for this is somewhat specious.[31] It was in eighteenth century Eastern Europe that it came to the forefront, since it was considered to be a real physical condition. Many thought that a vampire rose at night because of his intense sexual desires, satisfying them under the cloak of darkness. The only way a vampire could be rendered permanently dead was by driving a stake through his heart. Stoker took his cue from this mythology. But, strangely, he had his vampire come out in daylight, and his Dracula had no cape. The cape was added to the mythology in the 1931 movie *Dracula* (from the 1927 stage production) with actor Bela Lugosi. The belief that exposure to sunlight was fatal for the vampire was added to the evolving legend with *Son of Dracula* in 1941, starring Lon Chaney, Jr. Over the twentieth century, popular fiction gradually transformed Dracula into a suave nobleman, highly attractive and seductive, and fascinatingly dangerous. His bite on the female neck is erotic, as *Cosmopolitan's* survey corroborates. Like the legendary lover Don Juan, could Count Dracula be the unconscious sublimation of a fantasy figure—a secret erotic lover that women, at least in previous centuries, were expected to avoid as a danger to themselves (and by implication the social order), since he could turn them into ravenous sexual creatures? Linda Sonntag believes this to be so:

> The potent combination of eroticism and fear, blood and death, sends down many skeins of recognition into the unconscious mind. The kiss and the bite are both sexual. He comes at night to innocent maidens dreaming in their beds, ravishes them and leaves them bleeding, whereupon they are transformed into rampantly sexual beings. By day they remain pure and listless, but by night they become voluptuous harpies who in turn need the sexual kiss-bite to survive. [32]

Dracula symbolizes the breaking of taboos. He challenges authority and moralistic strictures. Aware of this symbolism, poets such as Wolfgang von Goethe and Samuel Taylor Coleridge took the vampire myth a step further, creating the first fictional female vampires in *The Bride of Corinth* (1797) and *Christabel* (1800) respectively. By expanding the narrative to allow women the right to express their erotic desires overtly, these writers tapped into the liberation of women subtext that the origin of the kiss entailed. In 1872, Sheridan Lefau created the first lesbian vampire in his novel *Camilla*—a novel that has inspired subsequent films, including Roger Vadim's *Mourir de Plaisir* (1962).

Whatever the symbolic meaning of vampirism, there is little doubt that it holds great appeal and stories about vampires today, like the *Twilight* series of movies, or television programs, like *Buffy the Vampire Slayer* and *True Blood,* reveal a new orientation in popular culture that has an estrogen tint embedded in it.[33] As Gregory L. Reece has written, vampirism characterizes what we seek in relationships perfectly:

> We are all "real vampires" in this sense. We all must constantly seek the sources of life, energy, sources of hope. We must create relationships in order to live, relationships with people willing

to give and willing to receive. And, like vampires, as quickly as the sun rises, we can turn to dust. Like vampires, without these things crucial for life, we will rot, slough off our skin, drop a bit of our nose, bloat with gases of decay, float in a pool of our own blood. [34]

The vampire myth is intertwined with moon symbolism and werewolves. The vampire storyline may thus reach back into even more ancient mythic traditions. In Greek legend, Lycaon was a wicked ruler who planned to murder Zeus. He did not succeed, and Zeus turned him into a werewolf. Werewolves have since appeared in many tales. In different versions, people turn themselves into wolves by putting on a wolf skin, by drinking water from a wolf's footprint, or by rubbing a magic ointment on their bodies. Or else, they are transformed into wolf monsters by someone else's magic power. In most stories, werewolves try to eat people, not just kiss them on the neck. [35] The most emblematic story of this kind is *Little Red Riding Hood*. In the original version, the little girl does not survive the wolf attack. She does, of course, in bowdlerized later versions. The people in the stories who are threatened by werewolves use various methods to bring them back to human form. These methods include saying the werewolf's real name, hitting the werewolf three times on the forehead, or making the sign of the cross.

A Conduit between the Body and the Spirit

The romantic lip kiss has, since its emergence, symbolized a conduit between the spiritual and the physical. This theme is found throughout the courtly love stories of the medieval era, turning them into the first true examples of a new and growing popular literature—a literature written about common people falling in and out of love and about love as an ideal. In these the kiss, if it is truly meaningful, allows the couple to live "happily ever after." Whether realistic or not, this ideal became the subtext of subsequent romantic narratives, turning ordinary men and women into princes and princesses in the popular imagination. In the nineteenth century *Briar Rose* fairy tale written by the Brothers Grimm the kiss of a prince awakens an entire kingdom and the couple lived happily together all their lives long. This idyllic "prince-kisses-beautiful-sleeping-female" story is an offshoot of the courtly love narrative. The woman is so beautiful that the male paramour cannot take his eyes off her. He stoops down and gives her a kiss. The moment he kisses her she opens her eyes and smiles at him. They leave together and all is set right again in the world.[36] The most emblematic, and well-known, version of this genre of narrative is the Sleeping Beauty tale.

The latter tale may actually derive form the *Volsunga Saga* of Norse mythology, where Brynhild may be the mythic proto-type of our Sleeping Beauty. She is portrayed as a strong, will-ful warrior goddess—a Valkyrie. Brynhild is placed in a ring of fire by her father after she pricks her finger, casting her into a long enchanted sleep. The hero Sigurd, with his hands stained by the blood of a dragon, draws Brynhild out of her sleep by putting his hands in his mouth. Then he places a ring on her finger. After this, he abandons her, and proceeds to marry someone else. Being a determined woman, Brynhild decides to take revenge on the faithless Sigurd and has him murdered. At his funeral she realizes that his death has not eradicated her love for him, and ultimately throws herself upon his funeral pyre in the hope of being reunited with him after death.

In a Sumerian version of the legend of Lilith the kiss plays a different, yet analogous role—it leads to death. To the Sumerians, Lilith was not only the goddess of fertility and ani-mals, but also a witchlike figure. In the story, she spurns the advances of a wayward prince, who had attempted to kill all the animals around her so that she would devote herself to him and him alone. But this action was counterproductive, since Lilith ended up weeping for the animals and befriending those who survived the onslaught. She mated with a serpent to spite the prince. From that sexual union a child with six arms and a serpent's tail was born. The child later fought night and day with the prince. Neither one emerged victorious from the duel. So, Lilith mated again and again with serpents, bearing 216 hybrid children. In fear, the prince ran away, swearing revenge. Afraid, Lilith turned herself into a great bird to flee the land, carrying people and animals on her back. When they came to dry land, the people built statues in Lilith's honor. They grew plentiful orchards, built buildings and towers of stone, growing wealthy. News of their wealth spread quickly. The prince got wind of all this, sending his heralds to make inquiries about its mysterious lady ruler. He then sent his army to conquer the people. But Lilith's serpent-children confronted the army and destroyed it. Realizing that the lady was Lilith, the prince went to her temple disguised as a woman. Seeing through the disguise, Lilith summoned 36 young men to protect her, at the same time calling for 36 beasts to be slaughtered for a great feast that she planned in order to trap the prince. People came from all over the land. The prince came too, as anticipated, disguised again as a woman. She welcomed him as an honored guest and then ordered him to marry one of the 36 men she had asked to come or else face death. Realizing what had happened the prince became enraged, ripping off his disguise: "Why are you making me marry this man?" She answered: "Because you can never marry me." The prince professed his love vociferously, claiming that he was prepared to cut his own throat if she did not give in to his demand. Having grown tired of this game, and feeling pity for the prince, she declared, "I will grant you one kiss." The desperate prince accepted the offer. So great was the pleasure of that one kiss that he died on the spot.

What is not clear from this story is what the kiss meant and how it was performed. Leaving such details aside, it is obvious that her kiss is more like a black widow spider's kiss—deadly—than a true lover's kiss.

The indirect, anecdotal evidence that the courtly love tradition liberated women from religious-based courtship strictures is abundant. In 1228, women first gained the right to propose marriage in Scotland, a legal right that then slowly spread through Europe. By the late 1800s, romantic love, not arranged courtship, became the primary requirement for marriage among most social classes.[37] An interested gentleman could simply walk up to a young lady and begin a conversation, although it was still expected that some time should elapse before it was considered appropriate for a man to be seen together with the woman. The kiss altered the cultural order, leading to the veneration of love in and of itself. The romantic kiss has led to the sexual revolution of the modern Western world. The effects of this revolution are everywhere, from television programs to movies of all kinds, which now deal openly with female sexuality, not attempt to hide it. The kiss, to put it in a different way, took the shame out of feminine love, allowing the latter to change the world. The rituals revolving around, or deriving from, the kiss show a blend of eroticism and romantic love. They are displays uniting the spiritual (sacred) and the sexual (profane). Freud connected the carnal part of love (ascribed to the god Eros in Greece) to the life instinct, which he called the Id; Carl Jung associated Eros instead with the feminine principle of life that he called anima, which he contrasted to Logos, the masculine principle of reason.[38] Jung elaborates his idea of Eros as a feminine principle as follows:

> Woman's psychology is founded on the principle of *Eros*, the great binder and loosener, whereas from ancient times the ruling principle ascribed to man is *Logos*. The concept of *Eros* could be expressed in modern terms as psychic relatedness, and that of *Logos* as objective interest.[39]

Agape is spiritual love. Starting in the courtly love tradition and ensconced in the new chivalric code (discussed above), the kiss unites Eros with Agape. The origin of the romantic kiss is, thus, one rooted in the need for union, between men and women, between the spiritual and the carnal; it is also one that loosened the shackles that Logos had established in the medieval world. It made romance a private act, between two lovers, not one that had to be acknowledged socially. To quote Frijhoff: "Even when performed in public, kissing and embracing are rites of appropriation and therefore of separation from the public sphere."[40] It also made sex intimate, meaningful, and thus, spiritual.

Today, the kiss has become itself an object-sign, to be revered on its own as if it were some kind of fetish. This is why there are now even "world kissing records." For example, one of the longest kisses ever recorded (to the present time) took place in New York City on December 5, 2001, between Louisa Almedovar and Rich Langley, lasting 30 hours, 59 minutes, and 27 seconds. A few years later, on September 1, 2007, in Bosnia, another record was set when 6,980 couples kissed for ten seconds. This was eclipsed on Valentine's Day, 2009, when 39,987 people came together in New Mexico locking in a kiss for ten seconds to the musical strains of *Besame Mucho*, the classic love song revolving around the power of the kiss. To date, the longest recorded kiss occurred in September 2010, between American students Matt Daley and Bobby Canciello, lasting for 33 hours performed in order to raise awareness for Gay rights. Incidentally, there is a Facebook site documenting French kissing world records. Every few months the French Institut Bonheur organizes a French kissing competition in different cities across the world, and recording the results on Facebook. It is interesting to note that a National Kissing Day was started a few decades ago in the UK, on July 6. This has now been adopted by the United Nations as International Kissing Day.

The whole discussion connecting the kiss with unfettered romance raises the more fundamental question of what is romance. We recognize it as a feeling. We have even given it mythic embodiments—Eros, Agape, Psyche, Cupid, and so on. But it seems to resist logical definition, and may even defy it. This is why it was expressed first in poetry and chansons. Émile Durkheim concluded that things like the emotions can only be understood through mythic figures of mind. These are expressions of the "collective conscious" of humanity that unites us all:

> The collective conscious is the highest form of the psychic life, since it is the consciousness of the consciousness. Being placed outside and above all individual and local contingencies, it sees things in this permanent and essential aspect, which it crystallizes into communicable ideas ... it alone can furnish the mind with the molds which are applicable to the totality of things and which make it possible to think of them.[41]

Romance is part of this collective conscious, and the lip kiss may well be the way we experience it in real life. This possibility was also entertained by Georges Bataille in 1957, who suggested that there is a chasm between the erotic and the romantic.[42] This chasm is bridged by the kiss. In their 1901 history of the kiss, Nyrop and Harvey were among the first to realize that the kiss may indeed have emerged to express a deeply embedded emotion.[43]

Clearly, the kiss tells us much more than is evident on the surface. It was, at first, an act of subversion, condemned by the religious authorities, because, as Kirshenbaum writes: "There was the very valid fear that kissing would lead to other sinful activities of the flesh."[44] But no one could stop its spread. In 1499 the Dutch humanist philosopher Desiderius Erasmus wrote about the kiss as an unstoppable "fashion" upon his return from traveling through England, obviously drawn by the "sweetness" of kissing, in which he had obviously engaged: "If you had once tasted how sweet and fragrant those kisses are, you would indeed wish to be a traveler, not for ten years, like Solon, but for your whole life."[45]

CHAPTER 3

The Kiss in Stories, Real and Fictional

We become lovers when we see Romeo and Juliet.
—Oscar Wilde (1854–1900)

Since its appearance as the maximal expression of romantic love in the chivalric literature of the medieval period, the lip kiss has migrated to all genres, from romantic novels to adventure stories where heroes and heroines are involved as much in romance as they are in bellicose escapades. As we saw in the previous chapter, some historians trace the custom of sending verses on cards on Valentine's Day to the letter written by St. Valentine to his paramour while he was in jail. Others trace it to a fifteenth-century episode connected with Charles, Duke of Orleans. He was captured by the English during the Battle of Agincourt in 1415, taken to England and put in prison. On Valentine's Day, he sent his wife a poem from his cell in the Tower of London telling her how much he loved her. Others still trace it to Chaucer's times, also as we saw. Whatever the case may be, it is obvious that romance seeks expression not only through the lips, but also through the written word.[1]

Writing poetry to a loved one has become an implicit practice in the enactment of romance since the spread of the chivalric code. This was a central theme in the movie *Il postino* (1994), directed by Michael Radford. A simpleton Italian postman learns to love poetry while delivering mail to the famous Chilean poet Pablo Neruda, who was exiled for political reasons.

Though poorly educated, the postman befriends Neruda. He is in love with a local beauty but struggles to express himself romantically to her. So, he seeks Neruda's help and guidance. The poet teaches him that the poetic instinct is innate and then advises him to let it dictate the fitting words to him through the feeling of love itself. The postman's beloved is called Beatrice, the name of Dante's great love. The allusion is transparent, since it was Dante who promoted the use of love poetry calling it part of an emerging dolce stil nuovo (sweet new style).

The view of the kiss as having the power to transform people's lives begins in medieval literary traditions. This theme has permeated the literature of love ever since. E. E. Cummings, one of the most innovative poets in modern-day American literature, known especially for violating the rules of punctuation and syntax, epitomizes the power of the kiss as connected to a woman's "profound and fragile lips" that open the path to the soul.[2] In the ideal of chivalric writing, kisses bind lovers, no matter what happens to them or to the world in which they live. That idea is now an unconscious theme in the popular imagination. There is no love story today without the kiss in a starring role, and if there were such astory, we would perceive it as strange, anomalous, or ironic.

Star-Crossed Lovers

The theme of star-crossed lovers making love under the moon at night became an *idée fixe* in medieval courtly love stories and poetry. No such *idée* had existed before in literature or art. The phrase "star-crossed lovers" was actually made popular by Shakespeare in *Romeo and Juliet*, to describe the most famous star-crossed lovers of history (Act 1, Scene 1, 58–59):

> From forth the fatal loins of these two foes,
> A pair of star-cross'd lovers take their life.

Today, the image of star-crossed lovers is everywhere in popular culture. Even role-playing video games feature them: Cloud

Strife and Aerith Gainsborough in *Final Fantasy VII* and Zero and Iris in *Mega Man X4*. A web-based soap opera, titled appropriately *Starcrossed,* has adapted the theme in a new way. In the program an astrologer separates the lovers experiencing troubles for one cycle of the moon, matching each one with another lover who makes a better astrological match. The idea is to fathom if the couples will succumb to the new partner or seek each other out again.

The star-crossed theme is likely an invention of the troubadours. Their praise of love, and their intense pining over it, stood in direct contrast to traditional Christian love, which was supposed to be controlled at all times, not passionate. The troubadours influenced many writers, including Dante and Petrarch. The image of a kiss under the stars or under a tree permeates their poetry. A perfect example is the following one, taken from a *canso* written by the troubadour Guillaume IX:

> If shortly I do not have the love of my good lady,
> I will die, by St. Gregory's head!
> Unless she kisses me in her room or under a tree.[3]

Guillaume emphasizes the saving power of his beloved's kiss, which represents the culmination of his happiness and the fulfillment of his desire. It must be performed in secret, hence in her room or under a tree. Bernart Marti, another troubadour, writes: "The power of the kiss to ennoble a lover is similar to the Platonic love where love of a human being can eventually lead to love of the divine."[4] Perhaps the best-known interpretation of the troubadour's romantic disposition is Giuseppe Verdi's magnificent opera *Il Trovatore* (1853), with its gloomy plot and powerfully passionate and dark musical score, recalling the many ill-fated love affairs of the historical troubadours.

The star-crossed troubadour, unable to appease his love, can only write about it. Unrequited love is the theme that infiltrates a large portion of the medieval courtly love literature.

A follower of this literary tradition, the medieval Italian poet Dante tells us in one of his writings that the most significant event of his youth was his chance meeting with Beatrice, the young woman with whom he fell desperately in love. She was his inspiration, turning to poetry to express his unconditional love for her. Dante's first important literary work, *La vita nuova* (The New Life), was written not long after Beatrice, the love of his life, died, leaving his love for her unrequited.[5] Combining verse and prose, it narrates the course his love had taken and his ultimate resolve to write a work that would be a worthy monument to her. That work was his masterpiece, *The Divine Comedy*.[6]

The image of two solitary lovers embracing under the stars, expressing unending love for each other, unable to fulfill their love because of forces beyond their control, is compelling. It is a story that does not end "happily ever after," but goes on forever in the imagination. Stars are symbols of destiny and fate. The expression "star-crossed" is an accurate one, because it implies that the stars participate in the two lovers' secret act of love, an act that will bring about dire consequences. The subtext here is that the kiss has the power to affect the world in unexplainable, if even tragic, ways. The kiss of a lover, or prospective lover, is too tempting to ignore—consequences be damned. The 1946 movie *The Postman Always Rings Twice* 1946, directed by Tay Garnett, underscores this very point. Two star-crossed lovers are driving along the highway. Frank (John Garfield) begs Cora (Lana Turner) for a long-awaited kiss, as she touches up her lips with lipstick. She promises him: "When we get home, Frank, then there'll be kisses, kisses with dreams in them. Kisses that come from life, not death." Frank responds: "I hope I don't wait." Unable to wait, they start to kiss. As they do so, Cora cries out frantically: "Look out, Frank!" Distracted by the kiss Frank runs off the road. The accident ends up killing Cora.

Stories of fatalistic love affairs are found before the medieval period. But they involved dangerous liaisons or illicit trysts among famous personages, not simple couples kissing under the stars. One such story is that of Jezebel, a Tyrian princess, daughter of Ethbaal, king of Tyre and Sidon (now in Lebanon). She became wife of Ahab, king of Israel, introducing the worship of the false idol and fertility god Baal to the Israelites, thereby evoking controversy and a scathing enmity from the religious leaders of the era. Unlike her bland female contemporaries, she stood out, coming across as a strong-willed, politically astute, and utterly defiant woman who dared to disregard the dictates of the society of her era had with regard to womanhood. Jezebel has been admired by writers across time, from Shakespeare and Shelley to Joyce. She also crops up as a recurring theme in contemporary popular culture, from Frankie Laine's hit single *Jezebel* to the 1938 movie *Jezebel*, starring Betty Davis.[7] Jezebel is a femme fatale—a sexually irresistible, but highly lethal, woman. The femme fatale theme has permeated popular culture, appearing in movies, best-selling novels, television programs, comic books, and video games. *La Femme Nikita* (1990), *Moulin Rouge* (2001), and *Femme Fatale* (2002) are just three examples of contemporary movies that treat this theme. The *Final Fantasy* video game series is populated with several femme fatales.

The male counterpart to the femme fatale is the philandering "love god." The legendary example of this figure is Don Juan, the brigand hero and unrepentant libertine. The original Spanish tale recounts the story of a promiscuous nobleman called Don Juan, whose ultimate mistake is to seduce the daughter of Seville's military commander. Not surprisingly, the legend originated in Europe during the Middle Ages. Its form became established in *The Trickster of Seville* (1630), by Spanish playwright Tirso de Molina. The handsome nobleman Don Juan Tenorio seduces women with great ease. But when he tries to seduce the daughter of the knight commander Don Gonzalo, the commander challenges him to a duel. Don Gonzalo is killed. Don Juan visits his tomb and scornfully invites the funerary statue of his victim to dinner. The statue appears at the feast and returns the invitation, which Don Juan accepts. In the graveyard, the statue takes Don Juan's hand and drags him down into hell as punishment for his crimes against God and society. The story has been dramatized by playwrights and put to music by composers throughout Europe, including by Mozart in his masterpiece, *Don Giovanni* (1787). Women in all versions of the Don Juan legend fell head over heels over this scoundrel, perhaps because he brought a sense of dangerous, and thus alluring, excitement in love matters. Loving an outlaw, gangster, or rascal is better than loving a staid, romantic-less person. As the rock group *Wham* put it in the 1980s, the love god is a "love machine." The best-known nonfictional love god of history was the Venetian Giacomo Giovanni Casanova. He was apparently irresistible to any of the women to whom he turned his attention, at least according to the legend. He himself recounts his amorous exploits in his *Story of My Life* (*Histoire de ma vie*), in which he reveals that he took some two hundred lovers, enduring imprisonment and even death, to do so.[8]

The basic star-crossed story differs from these kinds of stories in the fact that the two partners are madly in love with each other, not just attracted sexually, and prepared to withstand any opposition or contretemps in order to stay together, even if this means death. A contemporary movie that is based on this very theme is *Elvira Madigan* (1967), directed by Swedish director Bo Widerberg. It tells the story of an aristocratic army officer in Sweden who is prepared to give up everything, including his family, his career, and his social status quo, in order to run off with a beautiful circus performer. They decide to live together as outcasts, experiencing romantic bliss until the alienation and hardship of their life together brings their affair to a tragic end. Throughout the movie the couple performs many kisses. Each one is laden with tragic overtones, as the marvelous music of Mozart's twenty-first piano concerto in C Major (second movement) accompanies their embrace, emphasizing the tragedy just below the surface in its haunting melody.

Legendary Lovers

The theme of unrequited or impossible love actually has ancient roots, expressed in the form of myths and legends. These are being constantly reworked in contemporary popular culture, perhaps because they strike a powerful chord—the chord of love unfettered by social constraints and routines.

Two of the first lovers of mythic history were Orpheus and Eurydice. Orpheus was a handsome musician who was unrivaled among mortals for his attractiveness and musical talent. Orpheus traveled to the underworld to retrieve his dead wife, and love of his life, Eurydice. No mortal had ever been to the underworld. Moved by Orpheus's music, the ruler of the underworld, Hades, gave him Eurydice back on the condition that he would not look back at her until they reached the upper world. But Orpheus could not resist, and took a peek back just before stepping out, making Eurydice vanish. Heartbroken, he wandered alone in the wild until he was killed by a band of Thracian women, who threw his severed head into the river, where it continued to sing for his beloved Eurydice. After his death, the lyre he used to accompany himself became the constellation Lyra.

The Orpheus and Eurydice story is recycled throughout popular culture. It is found in all media, from the album *Abattoir Blues/Lyre of Orphaeus* (2004) of the alternate rock band Nick Cave and the Bad Seeds and folk artist Anaïs Mitchell's album *Hadestown* (2010) to Marcel Camus's 1959 film *Black Orpheus* and Neil Gaiman's comic series *Sandman*. Most of the adaptations of the story are set in a modern·context. *Black Orpheus*, for example, takes place in Rio de Janeiro during carnival. But in all recyclings it is the dark nature of the theme of love that can never be satisfied because of human foolishness that comes through. The characters in the mythic tale are part of an embedded thought pattern that may be deeply imprinted in Durkheim's collective conscious (previous chapter). This is perhaps why these stories are understandable and appreciated across societies, no matter what mythical themes they have been built on. From another, yet similar angle, one could say that they reflect Carl Jung's notion of archetype, which is a part of a collective unconscious (rather than conscious).[9] Jung believed that all humans share a level of mind, the unconscious, which contains universal thought patterns he called archetypes. These enable people to react to situations in ways similar to their ancestors. For this reason, Jung believed that the collective unconscious contains wisdom that guides all humanity. Archetypes are expressed in narratives, symbols, and rituals. Archetypal characters like the Joker, the Shadow, the Hero, and others, thus appear in different narratives, art forms, symbols, rituals, rites, metaphors, and discourses throughout history and across the world, but are understood in the same way. Modern-day representations of these three particular archetypes include stand-up comedians, Dracula, and Superman, respectively. Each one symbolizes a different psychic need—the need for laughter, the need to attenuate the power of fear, and the need to ensure the presence of valor in human affairs. They strike a responsive chord in us because they depict needs, vices, virtues, and elemental forces. The tragic lovers theme is an archetype in the Jungian sense.

Other archetypal examples of tragic lovers include Hero and Leander and Aphrodite and Adonis. Hero was the beautiful priestess of Aphrodite. She dwelt in a tower in Sestos, at the edge of the Hellespont (in Thrace, the ancient name for a large region in the Balkan Peninsula). Leander was a young handsome man from Abydos on the other side of the strait. He fell in love with Hero the instant he saw her and would swim across the Hellespont every night to be with her. She would light a lamp at the top of her tower to guide his way. This lasted through the hot summer. But, as in all such stories, the good times simply could not last. One stormy winter night, Leander was tossed by high waves into the sea while Hero's light was blown out by the breezes. Leander lost his way and was drowned. Hero plunged to her death from the tower in grief. This image of swimming across a river to seek fulfillment in love and life has appeared over and over ever since, with various adaptations. An interesting one is found in the 1959 pop song "Running Bear." Running Bear "a young brave," and Little White Dove "a young maid" are star-crossed lovers kept apart by the fact that they live in separate tribes who hate each other and a raging river that serves as a metaphor for their separation. The lovers dive into the river to be united in death, the song ending with "Now they'll always be together/In their happy hunting ground."

The goddess of love and beauty, Aphrodite, was the wife of Hephaestus, the god of metalwork. She had many lovers. It was to the handsome shepherd Adonis, though, to whom she gave her heart. But Adonis was also loved by Persephone, daughter of Zeus, who kidnapped and concealed him in the underworld. When he was accidentally killed, Aphrodite asked Zeus to restore Adonis to life and to her. Zeus decided, instead, that Adonis should spend the winters with Persephone in Hades and the summers with Aphrodite. But this unites the two lovers even more frantically. At one level, the myth provides a divine reason to explain why the seasons changed. But it does much more at an unconscious level. Love, betrayal, sex are all ingredients that reverberate in all of us. This is perhaps why the lovers in this myth have been recycled and refashioned ever since in poetry and prose. Interestingly, they have been utilized in psychology to describe various complexes. For example, the *Adonis complex* is used by psychologists as a term describing the obsession of preserving one's youthful body image, and the *Aphrodite complex* is used to refer to the deployment of a kind of feminine charisma that is based on a high-energy sexual power.[10]

As can be seen, this type of love story often involves betrayal, duplicity, perfidy, along with unrequited love on the part of both partners, despite the unfaithfulness. The most famous one comes from the Bible—the story of Samson and Delilah (Judges 16:4–20).[11] Delilah was Samson's Philistine mistress. He was an Israelite folk hero renowned and admired for his tremendous strength. The Philistines bribed Delilah to find out the secret of Samson's power so that they could take him prisoner. After a seductive dance, Samson revealed to Delilah that his strength lay in his long, thick hair which, because of a vow, he had never cut. Delilah shaved his head while he slept. When Samson awoke he found himself to be weak and helpless. The Philistines easily captured him, blinded him, and made him work as a slave. Delilah, however, had fallen madly in love with Samson, feeling remorse at what she had done, attempting to help him escape, but, of course, to no avail. As a story of betrayal and love, it has inspired artists such as Tintoretto and Antony van Dyck, and has been retold many times in popular culture, such as in the epic blockbuster movie, *Samson and Delilah* (1949), directed by Cecil B. DeMille. The story has also made appearances in television sitcoms and programs, from *Carnivàle* to *The Simpsons*. And it has inspired classical composers, such as Camille Saint-Saëns with his opera *Samson and Delilah* (1877). It has been the theme of many pop songs as well, including the Gershwins's *Samson and Delilah* (1930), from the musical *Girl Crazy*, and Tom Jones's *Delilah* (1968).

No list of ancient or classical lovers would be complete without including the doomed love affair between Cleopatra and the Roman statesman Mark Antony—a story that is part history, part myth. Cleopatra actually had love affairs with both Mark Antony and Julius Caesar. When Caesar arrived in Alexandria as a Roman general, he was instantly smitten by her amorous wiles, becoming her lover, restoring the throne that she had lost back to her. Cleopatra then moved in with Caesar in Rome as his mistress. After his assassination in 44 BCE, she went back home to Egypt. It was then that Mark Antony fell in love with her, moving to Egypt to be with her for the rest of his life. But Mark Antony eventually returned to Rome, where he married Octavia, a sister of Caesar's heir, Octavian. But he reunited with Cleopatra in 36 BCE, after conquering the Parthians, remaining in Egypt with her for several years, during which Octavian declared war against them. Following the Battle of Actium in 31 BCE, the lovers fled to Alexandria, where they both committed suicide.

Cleopatra personifies the prototypical femme fatale. She is described by Shakespeare in Act 2, Scene 2, page 12, of *Antony and Cleopatra* as follows:

> Age cannot wither her, nor custom stale
> Her infinite variety. Other women cloy
> The appetites they feed, but she makes hungry
> Where most she satisfies.

Maybe the first kiss was invented by Cleopatra after all, since history records that she enhanced her lip color with carmine (a vivid red color) and henna (a bright reddish brown), suggesting that she might have used her lips to seduce both Caesar and Antony. The story has certainly all the juicy elements in it that we still enjoy in stories about love, betrayal, and sex. There are versions of the tale in comic books (*Asterix and Cleopatra*, by René Goscinny and Albert Uderzo), musicals and ballets (*One More Gaudy Night*, 1961, by Martha Graham; and *Cleopatra*, 2000, by Ben Stevenson), film (*Serpent of the Nile*, 1953, directed by William Castle; *Cleopatra*, 1963, directed by Joseph L. Mankiewicz), popular music (*Cleopatra*, Danny Schmidt, 2005), games (Kheops Studio, *Cleopatra: A Queen's Diary*, 2007), television (*The Cleopatras*, BBC, 1983), and advertising (2010 TV ad campaign for Poise underwear featured Whoopi Goldberg as Cleopatra, and Subway's 2010 ad campaign featured Ewa Da Cruz as Cleopatra).

The ancient love stories may be the source of the courtly love tradition. The whole medieval period seems, in fact, to be marked as an era of lovers who can never satisfy their true love—because it went against the grain. The story of Troilus and Cressida was one of the first medieval versions of this storyline, appearing in the twelfth century, becoming famous after Shakespeare turned it into one of his best-known plays. According to the medieval story, which looks back in time to the last years of the Trojan War, Troilus, son of King Priam of Troy, and Cressida, daughter of a Trojan soothsayer, pledge eternal fidelity to each other. But during the Trojan War, Cressida is taken prisoner and eventually betrays Troilus, giving herself body and soul to Diomedes, a strong and handsome warrior. Troilus plots his revenge, but is killed himself. Does Cressida love Troilus or Diomedes, or both? The answer is never certain.

The story of Guinevere and Sir Lancelot du Lac is another medieval love tale filled with intrigue and dreadful consequences. Guinevere was the wife of the legendary King Arthur of Britain. She appears first in the *History of the Kings of England* cycle of Arthurian romances by English chronicler Geoffrey of Monmouth, circa 1136.[12] It was, however, the French poet Chrétien de Troyes who introduced the story to the world.[13] After marrying Arthur, Guinevere is smitten by Lancelot, a handsome knight of the court in Camelot. It is their adulterous relationship that eventually brings about the unraveling of Camelot and Arthur's downfall. Were Guinevere and Lancelot the model for the star-crossed lover theme that became so popular in the medieval ages? Their kiss is the fatal act that puts the tragic events in motion. It is described by de Troyes, as follows: "And the queen sees that the knight dares not do more, so she takes him by the chin and kisses him in front of Galahad for quite a long time."[14]

From the same Arthurian tale comes the legend of two other star-crossed lovers, Tristan and Isolde, retold over and over in many versions and forms. The story is about the knight Tristan who fell in love with the Irish princess Isolde, who was, however, betrothed to another man—King Mark of Cornwall. A love affair ensues between Tristan and Isolde. Mark seeks revenge. The two lovers escape to the forest where they live happily ever after. Was it love or lust that brought the two together? It depends on who the storyteller is. The story may predate, and have most likely influenced, the tale of Guinevere and Lancelot. It has had a substantial impact on Western art and literature since it first appeared. It was given musical expression, for example, by Richard Wagner in his eponymous opera of 1859. And it has been portrayed in movies, such as the recent 2006 film *Tristan & Isolde*, directed by Kevin Reynolds. In the movie version Tristan dies as a hero, with Isolde by his side. As Andrea Hopkins points out, these stories are consistent with the troubadour tradition of courtly love. They are stories that defy the marriage institution itself indirectly by suggesting that true love could hardly ever occur within marriage—a theme that has certainly permeated contemporary popular culture and may be the unconscious source of the drastic changes that the modern institution of marriage is constantly undergoing.[15] Hopkins suggests that the medieval tales of forlorn lovers laid the basis for the development of an unconscious code of behavior that made amorous trysts the antidote to boring arranged love unions.

Of course, the list of legendary lovers would not be complete without the story of Romeo and Juliet. It is *the* iconic story of star-crossed lovers. According to the Shakespearean version, the lovers belonged to two rival clans, the Capulets and the Montagues. Despite opposition from the families, they tied the wedding knot with the help of Romeo's friend, Friar Lawrence. Unaware of his daughter's marriage, Juliet's father decided to marry her off to Paris. Friar Lawrence advised Juliet to agree falsely to the marriage, since on the wedding day she would drink a harmless potion prepared by him that others would think was poison. The potion would only put her into a deep sleep, not kill her. People would believe that she had died; and a little later Romeo would come to rescue her. Juliet agreed. But the plan went awry, since Romeo was not informed in time about it. So, when he heard about his lover's death, he ended up taking his own life to join her in the afterlife. When Juliet awoke, discovering what had actually happened, she also took her life to unite with her beloved in death. The list of versions of the Romeo and Juliet story in popular culture would fill a large tome. Suffice it to say that it continues to represent the power of romantic love as a subversive act against the will of traditions and as a liberating force in the world of human folly, despite its tragic overtones.

There are, of course, different ways to interpret the Shakespearean story. Literary critic Stanley Wells looks at the contemporary sexual interpretations of such plays, wondering, however, whether these are not modern-day projections that Shakespeare himself may not have contemplated.[16] He also concludes, however, that there is a lot of sexual innuendo in the Shakespearean play, if one looks for it. In the past censorship was always a threat to playwrights, and thus they would reduce or eliminate the overt sexuality of passages such as the opening dialogue of the servants in *Romeo and Juliet*. Since the 1960s it has been common to restore the sexuality openly or to seek it out where it had not previously been suspected. This is done through setting, costume, and staging. There is certainly plenty of sex in Shakespeare, but in plays like *Romeo and Juliet* the focus is on the nature of unfettered love and its tragic repercussions.

The love affair between, Paolo and Francesca, as described in Canto V of the *Inferno* by Dante, epitomizes unrequited love. It recounts the true story of Francesca da Rimini, whose hand in marriage was given to Giovanni Malatesta to solidify the hard-won peace between warring families. Because her father knew she would reject the ugly and deformed Giovanni, his younger brother, Paolo, was sent as a proxy to retrieve Francesca. But she fell instantly in love with the handsome Paolo. Realizing that he was not her husband-to-be at her wedding, but that she was going to marry his brother Giovanni (Gianciotto in the *Inferno*) instead, she became enraged. Her love for Paolo could not be denied. According to Dante, the love was actually kindled after the two lovers had themselves read the story of Lancelot and Guinevere:

> One day, to pass the time away, we read
> of Lancelot—how love had overcome him.
> We were alone, and we suspected nothing.

And time and time again that reading led
our eyes to meet, and made our faces pale,
and yet one point alone defeated us.
When we had read how the desired smile
was kissed by one who was so true a lover,
this one, who never shall be parted from me,
while all his body trembled, kissed my mouth.
I fainted, as if I had met my death.
And then I fell as a dead body falls.[17]

The story's tragic ending comes when Gianciotto, rapier in hand, is about to kill Paolo. Francesca throws herself between the two brothers, trying to prevent the murder. But the blade passes through Francesca, killing her. Gianciotto, completely beside himself, for he loved Francesca more than life itself then strikes Paolo, killing him. The two lovers were buried in the same tomb, symbolizing their union beyond mortal life.

Paolo and Francesca's love story is overwhelmingly sad, because it depicts a love, sealed with a kiss, that transcends both life and death. Is death the fitting punishment for their misdeeds? Is a kiss disruptive of the routines that make up (or should make up) official courtship? As Juliet tells Romeo in the Shakespearean tragedy, "Then have my lips the sin that they have took," to which Romeo answers, "Sin from thy lips? O trespass sweetly urged!/Give me my sin again" (Act 1, Scene 5, p. 5).

Every culture has stories of tragic legendary and mythic lovers. From India to Arabia, from Africa to Asia, we find the same kinds of plots and characters. The details vary; the storylines do not. The common theme in all of them is that "ill-fated love" is perhaps the only truly achievable form of real love. Sinful, maybe, as Juliet says, but irresistible.

Celebrity Love Stories

The story of star-crossed lovers is an example of popular romantic literature. But the theme has crossed over into the realm of real life many times. Stories about celebrities who are involved in a doomed love affair abound throughout modern pop culture history. In some ways, the modern celebrity is a proxy of the mythic hero of the ancient and medieval worlds. Stories are told about celebrities in a parallel fashion, as larger-than-life figures whose actions are interpreted as more meaningful than the foibles of common people. In the contemporary context, a celebrity, however, need not achieve something heroic. He or she just has to achieve fame. As Daniel Boorstin defined the modern celebrity in 1961, the celebrity is "a person who is known for his well-knownness."[18] Like ancient mythic figures, some celebrities are remembered even after death.[19]

Perhaps the most famous of all celebrity love affairs is the one between the writer Georges Sand (the pen name of Amantine Lucile Aurore Dupin) and the great composer Frédéric François Chopin in the nineteenth century. She wanted him to remain with her forever; but he yearned to go back to his native Poland in a time of great upheaval there. With Sands he had settled into Majorca. One can still visit the monastery of Valledemossa there, where the two spent the winter of 1838–1839. Chopin was already ill with incipient tuberculosis, and by spending a winter in Majorca, he got worse. The two had not realized that winter in Majorca brought rain and cold. Chopin died only two years after leaving. The affair was as sad and agonizing as many of his magnificent piano works. Some believe that it was the inspiration for those works. The connection between his music and their love may, in itself, have been the impetus for the Romantic belief that the true artist could never settle down to marry, but would—given the idealistic nature of art—be condemned to suffering through unrequited or unachievable love.

One of the most common of all figures to emerge in the popular imagination is that of the "bad boy." The bad boy is a handsome, swashbuckling brigand, who lives a life of danger, yet rises above the masses, standing out as an ersatz heroic persona. This theme has gone beyond fiction, allowing historians and journalists to give various real-life love stories a dramatic reading.

Perhaps the most famous (or infamous) example is the Bonnie and Clyde story. Bonnie Parker and Clyde Barrow were star-crossed outlaw lovers, who, with their gang, pillaged parts of the central United States during the Great Depression. Their bank-robbing exploits and their love affair became the stuff of legend almost instantly throughout the country, capturing the attention of the American press during the so-called public enemy era between 1931 and 1934. The gang is also believed to have killed nine police officers and several civilians. They were eventually ambushed and killed in Louisiana by law officers. Both Bonnie and Clyde were in their twenties. The story is a classic one of a moll who becomes a partner in crime and in death, just so she could be with her bad boy. Its appeal inheres in the fact that it revolves around a life of danger, which is preferable to a life of boring routine to some (perhaps many) women. The gangster lifestyle holds a promise of excitement and, in the case of star-crossed lovebirds, unending romance, away from the probative and prying eye of society. Gangster lifestyle and romance make, together, a potent but perilous emotional brew. Actually, Bonnie may not have taken part in the violence, as some of the gang members later pointed out. She was simply smitten by Clyde and his lifestyle. A handsome outlaw, it would seem, exudes great sexual attraction. He is a dangerous hero, larger-than-life. He is under the control of the stars, not of men. Clyde was, and continues to be, the all-American rebel. Author Jeff Guinn, explains the enduring appeal of the Bonnie and Clyde story in his 2009 book *Go Down Together: The True, Untold Story of Bonnie and Clyde*, as follows:

> Although Clyde and Bonnie were never criminal masterminds or even particularly competent crooks—their two year crime spree was as much a reign of error as terror—the media made them seem like they were, and that was enough to turn them into icons. Barrow Gang fans liked the idea of colorful young rebels sticking it to bankers and cops. Clyde and Bonnie were even better than actors like Jimmy Cagney who committed crimes onscreen, because they were doing it for real.[20]

It is, as Guinn suggests, unlikely that the legend of Bonnie and Clyde was as exciting and romantic as the stories make it out to be. But we want it unconsciously to be that way. The legend mixes elements of the Robin Hood and Don Juan narratives, at the same time that it symbolizes America's rugged individualism and antiestablishment esprit.

The world of royals has had its share of star-crossed lovers, starting with the story of Napoleon and Josephine. Josephine was the beloved wife of Napoleon Bonaparte. She was born in 1763 and married the Viscount Alexandre de Beauharnais when she was 17. They had a son, Eugène, and a daughter, Hortense. The Viscount was one of the last victims of the French Revolution. Josephine was imprisoned for a time, narrowly escaping the guillotine herself. She soon became friendly with another Viscount, the Viscount de Barras, a government leader. Through his intercession, she got back some of her husband's estate, becoming shortly thereafter a leader in Parisian high society. It was at Barras's home that she met Napoleon. They fell immediately in love, marrying in 1796. They had no children. Josephine was beautiful, intelligent, graceful, and stately, making her an asset to Napoleon as he strived to climb the ladder of power. She was also naughty. Rumor had it that she had love affairs while Napoleon was on his military campaigns. These reached the emperor, enraging him. So, he decided to divorce her. She accepted his decision, promising never to doubt his love, and she took his suggestion to retire with imperial honors to Malmaison, a small estate near Paris that Napoleon had bought for her. Napoleon went on to marry Marie Louise of Austria in 1810. A son was born to them a year later. But the two original lovers could not let go of each other. When Napoleon was exiled to the Island of Elba, Marie Louise was not allowed to go with him. So, Josephine wrote a letter to Napoleon and asked permission to join him. He was forced to write back that it was impossible. Josephine died before his letter arrived.

Despite her betrayals, Napoleon was madly in love with Josephine, as reflected in the many love letters that have survived. In one letter he writes:

I awake full of you. Your image and last evening's intoxication have left my senses no repose whatever. You are leaving at noon; I shall see you in three hours. Meanwhile, mio dolce amor, a thousand kisses; but do not give me any, for they burn my blood. [21]

It is difficult to understand Napoleon's ardor for the emotionally shallow Josephine with her charm, bad teeth, unfaithfulness, and extravagances. But, as we saw in the previous chapter, romantic love is not guided by Logos but by Eros and Agape. These impulses clearly played out in the hearts of both Napoleon and Josephine.

The affair between Edward VIII and Mrs. Wallis Warfield Simpson has many parallels to this story. Less than a year after he was proclaimed King Edward VIII of the United Kingdom, Edward abdicated the throne in order to marry the divorced American Mrs. Simpson. He accepted instead the title of Duke of Windsor and his brother, the Duke of York, became King George VI. Edward's desire to marry a divorcée, while her two ex-husbands were still alive, brought about a constitutional crisis in Britain, which ultimately led to Edward's abdication in December 1936 so that he could marry his paramour. What could be a more romantic and star-crossed affair than this one? During World War II, the Duke and Duchess of Windsor were suspected of being Nazi sympathizers, adding even more intrigue to their story. But in this case, all's well that ends well, to use a Shaekespearean cliché. In the 1950s and 1960s, the lovers went back and forth between Europe and the United States, living a life of leisure as celebrities.

The love affairs of actors are now part of a new form of chivalric love—one that is spotlighted by Hollywood and other media shaping the popular imagination. An example was the tempestuous and often acrimonious love affair between the late actors Elizabeth Taylor and Richard Burton. They were married to each other twice; and they also divorced each other twice. Similar stories of love-gone-sour are those between Hugh Grant and Elizabeth Hurley and Tom Cruise and Nicole Kidman. Grant and Hurley met on the set of the Spanish movie,

Remando al viento, in 1987. Hurley then accompanied Grant to the premiere of the highly successful movie *Four Weddings and a Funeral* in 1994, in which he starred. Wearing a plunging black dress held together with gold safety pins, she caught his eye, as the story goes. They became a high-profile pair of lovers. It was during their romantic tryst that Grant became embroiled in an international scandal for soliciting the services of a female prostitute in 1995. However, in true star-crossed fashion, Hurley "stood by her man," as Tammy Wynette's 1968 hit country song puts it. But they split up five years later. Tom Cruise and Nicole Kidman became romantically involved on the set of their 1990 movie, *Days of Thunder,* and were married on Christmas Eve of that year. They adopted a daughter, Isabella Jane (born 1992), and a son, Connor Anthony (born 1995). They separated just after their tenth wedding anniversary. The reasons for the dissolution have never been made public. In June of 2006, Kidman stated in the *Ladies' Home Journal* that she still loved Cruise: "He was huge; still is. To me, he was just Tom, but to everybody else, he is huge. But he was lovely to me. And I loved him. I still love him."[22]

The star-crossed theme is a simulacrum—a state of mind whereby it is no longer possible to distinguish between fiction and reality, as French philosopher Jean Baudrillard termed it.[23] But the simulacrum is not a modern-day state of mind, as Baudrillard claims. It has always been that way. In the medieval period, people believed in the star-crossed stories of Tristan and Isolde or Lancelot and Guinevere in the same way that we relate to the love stories of celebrities. The theme is an archetype that stems from a deeply embedded belief in destiny. To this day, prospective love mates might go to a fortune teller to seek advice on their love lives, or read the horoscope to gain relevant insights. These are residual behaviors of an "astrology of love," as it may be called. Significantly, the word *astrology* means "study of the stars" and how they supposedly influence people's lives and events on the earth. This might reveal an unconscious perception of the world as controlled by unseen forces and, thus, that one's love fortunes are "written in the stars," or more to the point, "sealed by a kiss." As the Dutch Renaissance scholar, Daniel Heinsius, so aptly put it: "You may conquer with the sword, but you are conquered by a kiss."[24]

Romance Fiction

The word *fiction* was first used around 1412 in the sense of "invention of the mind." But fictional works involving romance became popular long before that with the rise of the long verse tale, the prose romance, and the Old French fabliau in the early medieval period, which, as discussed previously, emerged as part of a new and popular form of literature.

From the 1100s to the 1400s the romance story gained wide popularity, even though many historians of literature now believe that the eleventh century *Tale of Genji* by the Japanese baroness Murasaki Shikibu may have been the first true romance fiction novel, recounting the amorous adventures of a prince who wants to flee the staid lives of his descendants through love escapades.[25] The medieval romances dealt with knightly combat, adventure, and love trysts. The stories were called "romances," not only because they dealt with love, legitimate or otherwise, but also because they were written in the languages of the people, rather than in Latin (the official language of writing). Some claim that Geoffrey Chaucer wrote the first true romance story, *The Tale of the Tempestuous Whetnurse*, in 1395. However, Chaucer may have gotten his cue from Giovanni Boccaccio's collection of bawdy and romantic tales, called the *Decameron* (1351–1353), a book that tells of ten friends who take refuge in a country villa outside Florence to escape an outbreak of the plague. There, they entertain one another over a period of ten days with a series of stories that they make up for the occasion.

Horace Walpole's *The Castle of Otranto* (1764) was the first true Gothic romance, a genre in which lovemaking was enshrouded in a sense of mystery, terror, and the supernatural. The Gothic novels became instantly popular because of their emotionally irresistible blend of horror and romance, love and fear. The novels were called this way because they took place in gloomy castles built in the Gothic style. They had secret passageways, dungeons, and towers that provided the settings for strange and bizarre happenings and for secret star-crossed love affairs. Most were set in Italy or Spain, because those countries seemed remote and mysterious to English readers.

The style caught on throughout Europe, morphing into a new genre of novels, such as *Wuthering Heights* (1847) by Emily Bronte, that dealt with the dark side of romance.[26] In this masterpiece, the romance between Heathcliff and the young woman with whom he had been raised as an orphan boy, Catherine Earnshaw, is Gothic in its mood and setting, taking place in a foreboding place called Wuthering Heights. Madly in love with Catherine, Heathcliff flees the home after overhearing her say that it would be degrading for her to marry him. Catherine marries a wealthy gentleman named Edgar Linton. After becoming a rich and socially sophisticated man himself, Heathcliff comes back to Wuthering Heights, eloping with Linton's sister, as punishment to Catherine. Catherine eventually dies in childbirth, making Heathcliff carry with him a grief-striken sense of guilt for the rest of his life. The novel was condemned when it first appeared for its emotional bluntness, its lack of conventional morality, and its glorification of sexual passion. With its supernatural elements, and Heathcliff's pitiless cruelty, it caught on despite the censure. It has appeared constantly ever since in new editions of the book and in movies.

The late–eighteenth century writer Ann Radcliffe was the one who shaped the Gothic story into a formula, introducing supernatural intruders into the love scenes and the figure of the brooding villain, who often came disguised as a lover. Her novel *The Mysteries of Udolpho* (1794), became a best seller, leading to imitations and adaptations, such as the *roman noir* ("black novel") in France and the *Schauerroman* ("shudder novel") in Germany. In her last novel, *The Italian* (1797), Radcliffe's star-crossed lovers become ensnared in an arcane web of deceit spun by a malicious monk called Schedoni. They are eventually dragged before the Inquisition in Rome.

The Gothic genre spread broadly after the popularity of *Frankenstein* (1818) by Mary Wollstonecraft Shelley in England and Victor Hugo's *The Hunchback of Notre Dame* (1831) in France. Composers of the era were quick to transform the genre into musical works. Camille Saint-Saëns's *Danse Macabre* of 1874 comes instantly to mind, as does Franz Liszt's *Mephisto Waltz*es. The genre also influenced American writers like Nathaniel Hawthorne, Herman Melville, and Edgar Allan Poe. In the nineteenth century Jane Austen expanded it with her novel *Pride and Prejudice*, highlighting the emotional psychology of the female in a love partnership and not the exploits of a male hero.

The expansion of the genre to include more partners in a relation has come to characterize a large chunk of contemporary romance fiction. The modern fascination of the *ménage-à-trois* (or multiple partner) story starts with Avon Books' publication of Kathleen Woodiwiss's *The Flame and the Flower* (1972). Since then this subgenre has remained enormously successful. *Fifty Shades of Grey*, by E. L. James, is a case in point.[27] It is the story of a virgin who gives in romantically to a sadist, playing on the themes of vampirism and the bad boy at the same time, and becoming a pop culture craze for a while, complete with perfume, lingerie, jewelry, and a *Fifty Shades* logo. But women's erotic books are not new, and, in fact, it can be claimed that the early chivalric and romance stories, along with the courtly love and troubadour poetry, were as erotic as the current fare, and perhaps even more so because their eroticism was suggestive rather than explicit. The main characteristic of such narrative erotica is the presence of a strong female personage—a woman grappling with her own sense of sexuality and womanhood.

As Janice Radway argues, romance fiction is a perfect vehicle for women to understand their sexuality on their own terms.[28] Women readers understand the various formats of the romance and gladly become engaged with them, because it allows them to think reflectively about love, sexuality, marriage, and motherhood. Such reading constitutes female empowerment, not victimization (as some acerbic critics have claimed).

The romance and the fairy tale have a lot in common. Indeed, some of the more memorable kisses of all time come from the fairy tale, including those that are showcased in the Sleeping Beauty and Cinderella stories. Taking place in a surreal world filled with magic and unusual characters, fairy tales hold a strange magical appeal over every child, no matter what age. They tell of an underdog hero or heroine who is put through a great trial or must perform a seemingly impossible task, and who, with magical assistance, secures his or her birthright or a perfect marriage partner. Such stories begin with "Once upon a time" and end with "And they lived happily ever after," formulas that give us a sense of true love as being eternal, unlike everything else in human life.

A fairy, in folklore, is a diminutive supernatural creature who typically has a human female form and lives in an imaginary region called a fairyland. She intervenes in the world, in order to help humans in some way. The sirens in Homer's *Odyssey* are fairies, and a number of the heroes in the *Iliad* have fairy lovers in the form of nymphs. The gandharvas (celestial singers and musicians), who figure in Sanskrit poetry, were fairies, as were the hathors, or female genies, of ancient Egypt, who appeared at the birth of a child and predicted the child's future. Fairies appear in Shakespeare's *A Midsummer Night's Dream* and *Romeo and Juliet* (in Mercutio's "Queen Mab" speech), *The Faerie Queene* by Edmund Spenser, *L'Allegro* and *Comus* by John Milton, *Tales of Mother Goose* by Charles Perrault, *Grimm's Fairytales,* by the brothers Jacob and Wilhelm Grimm, and *Irish Fairytales* by William Butler Yeats.

The good fairies are sensitive and tender, but they are also capricious, inclined to play pranks. The bad fairies are responsible for such misfortunes as the bewitching of children; the substitution of ugly humanoid creatures, known as changelings, for human infants; and the sudden death of animals. The quintessential fairy in contemporary popular culture is Disney's Tinker Bell. But she is not your average fairy—she tried to kill Peter Pan's pal Wendy in a jealous rage. But we still like her because of her sassy attitude and appealing tender looks. Fairy stories were once passed on by word of mouth. It was a Frenchman named Charles Perrault who wrote them down, publishing them in a book called *Tales and Stories of the Past with Morals: Tales of Mother Goose* in 1697.[29] The collection included *Sleeping Beauty, Cinderella, Red Riding Hood*, and *Puss in Boots*. The story of Cinderella has had particular appeal to the movie-going generation, starting with Disney's 1950 animated version and morphing into more recent renditions with titles such as *Ella Enchanted* (2004) *The Prince and Me* (2004), and *The Cinderella Story* (2004). In the latter, it is a lost cellphone that leads Prince Charming to the girl, not a misplaced glass slipper. The former (*Ella Enchanted*) is a spoof of the tamer Cinderella characters of the past. The title character wants to free herself of the curse of obedience, to become independent and free of the enslaving past.

In all such stories the kiss plays a central role. The kiss itself has been portrayed as the power behind the romance in stories titled simply *The Kiss*, which have been written by famous authors, including Anton Chekhov (1887), Kate Chopin (1895), Kathryn Harrison (1997), and Danielle Steel (2002). Many stories today, from adventure to mystery narratives, simply would not be complete without a love plot or subplot to them. And such a subplot would make no sense without kissing. The kissing scene in narratives and in real life constitutes a social performance of romance, especially in its initial stages. This is why we sweeten our breath and brush our teeth before kissing. Nature would never tell us to do this. Indeed, it would appear that our ancestors liked the "natural odor" of the human breath. We have developed a kind of "cosmetic hygienics" over time because of the meanings of the kiss. Certainly advertisers know this better than most of us. Already in the 1920s, Pepsodent toothpaste mounted an ad campaign whose slogan put it appropriately as follows: "Magic lies in pretty teeth." The ads showed a man and a woman seated at a restaurant, looking at each other romantically. The subtext was, clearly, "Brush your teeth with Pepsodent and, magically, you will improve your romantic life."[30]

As Karen Harvey has shown, there is no one theory of kissing.[31] A certain type of kiss might be a key to the past of a culture, it might have great symbolic value, or it might play a role in various courtship rituals. The relationship between love and sex, or Agape and Eros, is a complex one. The romance novel genre certainly understands this. Love may exist without sexual desire or vice versa. Nevertheless, the feelings of being in love with, and sexually attracted to, another person are frequently intertwined. For most of the twentieth century, the theory of the "family drama" put forward by psychiatrist Sigmund Freud dominated theories of romance and sexual relationships.[32] Freud believed that the adolescent's choice of mates was largely determined by his or her childhood experiences and relations with the parent of the opposite sex. For Freud, every child had an unconscious desire for sexual attachment with the parent of the opposite sex. If the attachment is between a male child and the mother it is called the Oedipus complex, from the myth of Oedipus, a Greek hero who unknowingly killed his father and married his mother. Later researchers used the term "Electra complex" for the same complex in girls, since according to Greek legend, a woman named Electra helped plan the murder of her mother. Does this mean that we end up searching for a mate who resembles our parents? How would we explain the fact that some women are attracted to "bad" men, such as outlaws, gangsters, philanderers, and the like, and some men to philandering and dangerous women? Is that because their parents were bad? I see in these escapades, or "dangerous liaisons," the lure of adventure, of unending romance, unfolding in a constant state of danger and thus excitement, not any psychological complex.

CHAPTER 4

The Kiss in Images

Every young sculptor seems to think that he must give the world some specimen of indecorous womanhood, and call it Eve, Venus, a Nymph, or any name that may apologize for a lack of decent clothing.

—Nathaniel Hawthorne (1804–1864)

The myth of Pygmalion is a fascinating one on many levels. Pygmalion, king of Cyprus, was a renowned sculptor. Disgusted by what he saw as the wicked women of his day, he sculpted an ivory statue of what he envisioned to be the ideal woman—beautiful, virtuous, kind, and intelligent. After sculpting it, he fell madly in love with his own creation. He wanted to make love to her. So, he implored the goddess of love and beauty, Aphrodite, to turn his statue into a living human being. The goddess granted Pygmalion his wish, bringing her to life as Galatea. Pygmalion married Galatea and, together, they had a son named Paphos. This tale has intrigued many writers, from the Roman poet Ovid, who retold the story in his *Metamorphoses*,[1] to George Bernard Shaw, who rewrote it in the form of his play *Pygmalion* (1913), which tells how an English gentleman (a professor of phonetics) makes an elegant lady out of a poor ill-bred girl by teaching her to act and speak with proper grammar and pronunciation.[2] The musical comedy *My Fair Lady* (1956) was based on Shaw's play. Was there kissing in the original Pygmalion story? Some versions of it seem to indicate that there was. But this might again be a case of retrofitting, that is, of evaluating and interpreting the past in terms of the present.

The kiss has been the subject not only of poets and narrators, as we saw in the previous chapter, but also (and especially) of visual artists—painters, sculptors, and photographers. They have provided us, through the centuries, with many ways of literally "viewing the kiss." In each image, however, there is a level of representation that imbues the kiss with layers of meaning. An example that comes instantly to mind is the 1908 painting by Austrian nouveau style artist Gustav Klimt, a painting that brings out the kiss's delicate romantic and passionate qualities at once.[3] The kiss seems to morph before our eyes into a permanent etching of love—love cast in stone. The lovers are kissing on the edge of a flowery precipice, their bodies pressed together in a tender embrace. The man presses his lips against his lover's cheek, not her lips, which emphasizes the tenderness of the act. She offers him her tilted head in a state of ecstatic abandon. He wears an all-enwrapping gown made of black and white rectangles and squares, which forms a sharp contrast to her gown full of colors and concentric circles. We can only see the back of his head while her face is visible. The male figure is the initiator of the kiss, she the willing receiver. The two seem to be in a cocoon, with the kiss insulating them from the vagaries and tribulations of everyday banal life.

Other famous painters who made the kiss the object of their creative fancy are among the greatest of all time. These include Titian, Rubens, Canova, Munch, Schiele, Chagall, Matisse, Toulouse-Lautrec, Rodin, and Hayez, to mention but a handful. Add to these Rodin's overpowering *Kiss* sculpture, the Times Square photo of a returning sailor kissing his nurse paramour, and virtually all of advertising's images promoting the sale of cosmetic products, such as lipsticks and perfumes, and we can build a "pictography" of the kiss across the artistic and commercial landscapes. The visual story of the kiss underscores its ensconcement in the domain of the popular as the perfect symbol of romance.

Painted Kisses

It is impossible to imagine human life without visual art. From the ad posters we see on a subway platform to the priceless paintings hanging in an art gallery, the art instinct leaves its residues all around us. For some, like New Zealand philosopher Denis Dutton, it is as natural for us to instinctively look at an art work as it is to squint our eyes when something comes near them.[4]

Archeologists trace the origin of art to the Old Stone Age (20,000 to 15,000 BCE). The paintings found on cave walls from that era are enigmatic works, since no one really knows what they meant or what function they exercised in early social life. They are not just simple reproductions of animals or people; they are interpretations, providing a perspective on the world through the eyes of the artist. According to Plato, the eyes of the sculptor sees an image in a formless slab of marble, giving it physical shape with the hands and the imagination. The world changes as a consequence when that shape is brought into existence. Traditionally, artists were considered employees of the aristocracy or the clergy. Sumerian priests and Renaissance princes or financiers alike were the ones who hired artists for their own purposes and provided sufficient wealth to enable them to work comfortably, as long as they produced works that they requested. The Romantic Movement changed all this, emphasizing individualism, free from patrons and sponsorship. The view of the artist as an eccentric genius impelled by his or her own creative energies, free of the yoke of social norms or practices, is very much a product of this movement.

Images of kissing can be found in Etruscan art. One work dates back to 480 BCE and it is a homosexual kiss, performed between Erastes and Eromenos (older and younger lovers). Is this the first romantic kiss? Is it the forerunner to the popularized romantic kiss as we have known it since the medieval period? To the best of my knowledge, no one has given that painting a definitive interpretation based on archeological and historical evidence. It may have been a kiss of love and union, but it is unlikely to have the same meanings as the romantic kiss that emerged in medieval times.

It was in the Renaissance, a little after the courtly love literature had spread through European society at large, that depictions of the kiss in art started proliferating. Among these, Agnolo Bronzino's *Venus, Cupid, Folly, and Time* (c. 1545), commissioned by Cosimo de' Medici of Tuscany for King François I of France, shows how Renaissance painters began to reinterpret the mythic past with new eyes.[5] In the painting, Venus sits naked, her knees bent and her back arched, while her son, Cupid, kneels to her left with the top of his torso behind her body. Their kiss is delicate and intimate, rendered graceful by the physical closeness of their bodies as well as Cupid's hands modestly covering Venus's breast. But there is a jarring, or at least anomalous, image in the scene that stands out vividly. Venus appears to be sticking her tongue out, and Cupid's lips seem to convey sexual excitement. Was this the precursor to the French kiss? Is this folly, as the title of the painting suggests? Does it portray filial love forming the basis for later romantic love, as Freud was to proclaim centuries later? Do men really search for a woman to replace the mother's kiss, transforming it from a filial to an erotic one? Interestingly, there is a father figure at the top of the scene extending his hand forward in an attempt to touch Venus. Is he trying to stop this? Whatever the interpretation of this painting, there is little doubt that the kiss emerged as something much more than a courtly love gesture, playing a suggestive role in calling attention to the hidden psychology of human relations. This is a remarkable hidden gem in the history of the painted kiss.

One of the most passionate kisses captured on canvas is the one in *Hercules and Omphale* (c. 1730) by French rococo artist François Boucher.[6] According to Greek legend, Hercules was the slave to Omphale, queen of the kingdom of Lydi. In captivity he falls for her. The kiss in the painting between the two is erotic yet also romantic, performed with arms and legs intertwined. She exudes great power, with her arm draped around his back and her leg over his. Hercules's arms grapple her breasts and her back. But their embrace is somehow tender and seemingly indissoluble. It looks as if it will go on forever. The painting is a celebration of romance, passion, and desire, taking place before an audience of small cherubs. Does this suggest that kissing is angelic and spiritual, even if it has sexual intent?

Jean Auguste Dominique Ingres's 1819 painting of star-crossed lovers, *Paolo and Francesca*, dramatizes the sway of the furtive kiss to change people's lives and chart their destiny from that moment onward.[7] The painting captures the moment when the two legendary lovers kiss in secret as Paola's husband, Gianciotto, arrives unexpectedly, catching the two lovers in the act. This is a visual portrait of the dual meaning of the act of secret kissing—passion and betrayal. Paolo is clearly the initiator, leaning his body into Francesca as she angles her face away from him. It is unclear whether she is partially rejecting his kiss or quietly accepting it and what her motivation is for doing so. It is interesting that Paolo ends up actually kissing her neck, not her lips, as he embraces her possessively. The colors of their clothing are also notable. The young couple wears flashy, fashionable garments, while Gianciotto stands, sword drawn, in the background in a gloomy dark robe. The contrast is stunning and stark, mirroring the moral ambiguity of secretive kissing itself.[8]

In Francesco Hayez's 1859 painting titled *The Kiss* the male is depicted with a flowing cloak, large hat, concealing a substantial amount of dark brown hair, which gives him a suave and captivating appearance, although his face is hidden away from sight. The face of the female figure is only partially exposed, accentuating the secret nature of kissing. The painting also outlines sexual differences in the performance of the kiss. The man appears dominant, leaning over the woman, with his hands cupping her face and hair. She is a willing party as can be seen by the fact that she has her hands on his shoulder. The kiss appears stolen, or against the wishes of someone (the woman's husband or the man's wife?), taking place in a darkly lit stairway.

Pygmalion and Galatea by Jean Léon Gerome (1890) revisits the myth of Pygmalion.[9] As discussed, Pygmalion loathed all women, but being lonely he decided to carve the "perfect woman" out of marble. Galatea was his "angel woman," to borrow an image of womanhood from the courtly love poetry tradition, and he fell deeply in love with her, dressing her and speaking to her. During Aphrodite's annual festival, Pygmalion went to her altar and implored her to turn Galatea into a flesh and blood woman. Aphrodite heard his heartfelt plea and when Pygmalion returned home and kissed Galatea, as Gerome suggests, her lips were not ivory but warm, soft, and alive. The couple instantly fell in love. The painting depicts Pygmalion and Galatea's first kiss—she, still partially made of ivory, leans her naked body over his, while he clasps her back with his arms. Theirs is a kiss of awakening. Through the kiss a lifeless woman has been given life. As Paula James argues, the myth has proven to be inspirational for writers, artists, philosophers, scientists, directors, and creators of films and television series because it deals with the power of womanhood to literally come alive through the kiss.[10]

Edvard Munch's *The Kiss by the Window* (1892) shows two lovers pressing their bodies together into a perfect indissoluble embrace.[11] Munch's impressionist blending of colors adds to the mystical effect produced by the embrace. When two people kiss intimately, they become one. This blending is also evident in his kiss etching of the same year where the lovers' faces morph into a mass. René Magritte's great painting of two lovers (*Les Amants*, 1928) constitutes an intriguing mysterious portrait of the act of kissing, since both faces are covered by a shroud of some type. It seems to ask: Why do we do this? Or does the painting symbolize the idea that love is blind and that lovers can recognize one another without looking at each other? On the other hand, does it perhaps suggest the universality of this romantic gesture, as borne out by the fact that both lovers and their setting have no perceivable identity? Or are they wearing death shrouds that imply that love transcends death (see figure 4.1)?

Figure 4.1 *The Kiss by the Window* (René Magritte, 1928)
(*Source*: National Gallery of Art open access images)

The series of comic book style paintings by the late New York pop artist Roy Lichtenstein are truly interesting, providing a modern depiction of the kiss. His 1962 painting, *The Kiss*, plays visually on the various meanings imprinted by modern-day society into the act of kissing. Is the dashing young man, presumably a pilot (suggested by his cap and a plane in the background), coming or going? Is his a parting kiss or does it depict the pleasure of returning home to the woman? She appears to be a vixen—blonde haired, wearing a red dress, red nail polish, and bright red lipstick. But instead of kissing him squarely on the mouth, she is leaning back below him, and seemingly swooning with pleasure at his neck kiss. Both have their eyes closed, which heightens the emotional power of the kiss.

Later that year, Lichtenstein painted *Kiss II*, featuring two young adolescents in a passionate, fiery embrace, suggesting that something is about to explode during kissing. Two years after that, in 1964, he painted the masterpiece in the set, *Kiss V*. The woman is shown with bright red lips, drawing our attention impellingly to them, much like the emphasis on the female lips in advertising. The kiss is yet another neck kiss. Her mouth is pressed against his cheek, indicating a perfect mixture of sensuality and romance. Depending on which way the image is rotated the kiss seems to communicate parting and loss, or return and joy. As several critics have pointed out, Lichtenstein's work defined the basic premise of pop art better than any other by using comic book techniques, allowing him to produce hard-edged, precise paintings that both raised and satirized deep questions, such as the nature and expression of romance.[12]

Finally, American psychedelic artist Alex Grey's 1983 painting, *Kissing*, strikes us by its uniqueness, focusing on the inner musculature structure of two kissers during the performance of the act. The two kissers are shown through an X-Ray image, making them seem to blend into the background. The painting might suggest the interconnectedness to the world and to each other that lovers feel while they kiss.

As the foregoing sampling of paintings suggests, the kiss is powerful—emotionally and socially. It changes things. The late pop artist, Andy Warhol certainly understood this perfectly. In 1963, he filmed his friends and acquaintances kissing in unbroken, four-minute-long shots. The result was a series called *Kiss*, which took the art and cinematic worlds by storm with the transformative power that exuded from the kisses—the lips, the tongue, and the other anatomical parts involved in kissing constituted a text, cohering together seamlessly.

Sculpted Kisses

An anonymous sculpture in the Chitragupta Temple, dating back to circa 1000 CE, is probably the first sculpture depicting the mouth-to-mouth kiss in history, again suggesting that the origin of the romantic kiss may be in India a century before it emerges in Medieval Europe, as discussed previously. If that kiss is indeed romantic (and not solely sexual), then it could well have been the prototype kiss that surfaces in other parts of the world later. The sculpture is dedicated to Surya, the

Sun God. It prefigures other and subsequent kiss sculptures. Whatever its meaning, it brings out the fact that sculptors, like painters, have also been fascinated by the kiss. Sculpture allows the artist to give the act a three-dimensional form, literally bringing it out into real space, for all to see and touch.

The masterpiece sculpture of the kiss is undoubtedly Auguste Rodin's marvelous 1886 sculpture, titled the *Kiss*, which casts into marble the story of star-crossed lovers Paolo and Francesca (see figure 4.2). It is one of the most famous art works of all time, with the two lovers portrayed in the nude.

The sculpture was originally intended to be part of the *Gates of Hell*, a bronze portal commissioned for a planned museum of art in Paris in 1889. Rodin did not feel that the image of the

Figure 4.2 *The Kiss* (Auguste Rodin, 1886)
(*Source*: National Gallery of Art open access images)

two lovers fit into the scene and so he removed them, making an individual statue of them. Rodin described his sculpture as, "complete in itself and artificially set apart from the surrounding world."[13] The kiss is impassioned and wild. The lovers appear to be equally overwhelmed by the kiss, suggesting intense passion at the same time that their nudity implies intimacy. A bronze version of the sculpture (74 centimeters high) was sent for display to the 1893 World's Columbian Exposition in Chicago. It was deemed unsuitable for general public viewing and relegated to an inner chamber with admission only to adults.[14]

Psyche Revived by Cupid's Kiss (1787) by Antonio Canova focuses on the life-giving power of the kiss. In the sculpture the kiss has not taken place yet. It shows a "soon-to-be" kiss between Cupid and Psyche, after Psyche had regained Cupid's love, but is under an enchanted spell. The near-kiss is intimate and tender, and fraught with anticipation. They seem to be gazing into one another's eyes, as Psyche runs her fingers through Cupid's hair and his arms cradle her head and breasts. As we saw, in Roman mythology, Psyche was a devastatingly beautiful princess who made the goddess Venus jealous of her beauty. In one version of the story, Venus ordered her son, Cupid, to make Psyche fall in love with the ugliest man in the world. Instead, Cupid fell in love with Psyche, but he forbade her to look at his face. When she did, he abandoned her. They were eventually reunited. The sculpture depicts the reunification scene. The technique of anticipation in the sculpture is the same as the one used in movie scenes—when the lips of the two lovers come close, but do not kiss, we become anxious, on edge, setting us up for the "emotional catharsis" that the kiss provides.

Romanian sculptor Constantin Brancusi's *The Kiss* (1908) is effective because of its stark simplicity.[15] The focus is not on the lovers, but on the act of kissing itself, capturing the essence of the act. Rather than recognizable faces, the sculpture shows two abstract figures, locked in an eye-to-eye, lip-to-lip, and body-to-body embrace (see figure 4.3). The figures are mirror

Figure 4.3 *The Kiss* (Constantin Brancusi, 1908)
(*Source*: National Gallery of Art open access images)

images of one another, suggesting spiritual and physical union or even fusion. The kiss, the sculpture proclaims, is an inextricable bond, turning two hearts into one. The identity of the kissing partners is irrelevant. It is the kiss that counts.

Finally, *Yuanyang II* (2007), by contemporary Hong Kong sculptor Tsang Cheung Shing is among the most interesting contemporary visual interpretations of kissing. The title of the sculpture refers to a Chinese elixir of love drink that is made by mixing coffee and milky tea. The shades of light and dark spill out of the mugs containing the Yuanyang elixir over the faces of the two lovers as they kiss passionately. Eyes closed, noses touching, and lips pressed against one another, the two are locked in a magical embrace, oblivious to what is going on around them. The use of contrasting colors is also suggestive of the Chinese philosophy of yin and yang, and thus of the balancing of energies, male and female, as they mesh in the act of the kiss.

Photographic and Iconic Kisses

In March 1956 a young photographer was assigned to take pictures of an upcoming young singer known as Elvis Presley. The photographer was Albert Wertheimer. His photo shocked the world and was rarely shown after Elvis became a superstar, the king of rock and roll. The reason is obvious. Elvis and the young woman are performing a very erotic version of the French kiss—a photo that the moralism of the era would hardly have allowed to get out into public view. The shock effect kept it out of the public eye for years. Wertheimer went on to snap some of the most famous, spontaneous, behind-the-scenes photos ever taken of Elvis.

Photography became an art form almost from the instant the technology was invented. From the 1860s through the 1890s some portrait artists used it as an alternative to drawing and painting, since it allowed for greater fidelity of representation. Today, photography is a full-fledged art of its own. Photos provide visual proof that we do indeed exist in some form, not just in our minds. This is why in Michelangelo Antonioni's 1966 movie masterpiece, *Blow-Up*, the search for clues to a crime in a blowup of a photograph is a metaphor for the search for clues to our own existence in our photographic images. A successful mod photographer in London whose social world revolves around fashion, pop music, marijuana, and easy sex, starts suffering from existential ennui, feeling that his life is boring and meaningless. He takes uninspired fashion photos, and is cruel to his models. His life changes when he meets a mysterious beauty. He does a photo shoot of her in a park, noticing something frightful—a corpse—in the blowup of one of the photos in his darkroom later. The fact that he may have photographed a murder scene does not occur to him until he studies the details of the negatives, blowing up smaller and smaller components, and finally putting the puzzle together. Because of his discovery he becomes inspired again, searching for meaning to life in the meaning of the crime-scene photo. He does not find it, but the search itself is what is intriguing and what gives him new vitality. The movie also shows one of the most erotic kisses of cinematic history, between the photographer and his beautiful woman (played by Vanessa Redgrave). The link to the mystery of kissing is transparent. Love, sex, and life all come to an end, as if there was nothing to them in the first place.

One of the most famous photos of the kiss is the one by photographer Alfred Eisenstaedt showing a sailor kissing a nurse on August 14, 1945, in Times Square during a celebration of America's victory over Japan, published in *Life* magazine. It has become so iconic that prints of this kiss can be found in households and offices across America. No one really knows who the kissers were, but dozens have since come forward to claim the honor. While the mystery will probably never be solved, Eisenstaedt has left us with a juicy background story about the male kisser. In his autobiography, the photographer writes that he followed around a sailor who moved through the crowd, kissing anyone wearing a skirt.[16] Our famous sailor therefore turns out to be a philanderer, rather than a romantic boyfriend or husband, as we imagine, or want, him to be. The power of this kiss catches us off guard, especially since kisses of this type hardly ever get performed in public. The photo was plastered all over the newspapers, being seen as a symbol of a new era of peace, love, and hope.

Challenging the popularity of Eisenstaedt's photo is Robert Doisneau's *Le Baiser de l'Hotel de Ville* (The Kiss at City Hall), Paris, 1950. Doisneau worked as a commercial and industrial photographer. His photographs of the liberation of Paris after World War II were published worldwide, appearing in countless newspapers and magazines. But it is his *Le Baiser de l'Hotel de Ville* photo of two lovers stealing a kiss on a crowded Paris street that has become one of the most reprinted images on postcards, notecards, posters, and Internet sites. The setting is similar to the Eisenstaedt photo, with people moving about. But the couple in the Doisneau photo appear to be kissing in a much more traditional, and even less passionate, way. What makes the photo romantic is the fact that the couple performs the act with closed eyes and in public, defying social mores and emphasizing romance at any cost. Incidentally, during a lawsuit against the photograph, Doisneau admitted that the photo did not catch a spontaneous fleeting moment in time, but was actually staged. Of course, this does not matter to viewers who nonetheless see in it the promise of romance that a kiss evokes.

Several photographs have become central to the modern history of pop culture. One of these is the photo of Marilyn Monroe blowing a kiss to an imaginary audience, even though it does not show her in an embrace with a specific partner. The photo is powerfully enticing because it is we, the viewers, who are her partners. The date and photographer are unknown, but whoever it was, he or she gave us a visual portrait of the kiss that is truly evocative, blending romantic expectation with anticipation of sexuality from an icon of the 1950s. Another photographed kiss that has become emblematic in the annals of pop culture history is the one captured by Annie Liebovitz of Yoko Ono and John Lennon kissing in bed in 1980. The photo was used as a *Rolling Stone* magazine cover. The vulnerability of two rock heroes is what makes the photo so intriguing and emotionally potent. Lennon's nudity is in stark contrast with Yoko's dark clothing, conveying a sense of maternal love as she cuddles her mock "fetus." Given what occurred shortly thereafter, with Lennon being murdered on a Manhattan street, the photo is even more moving when viewed years later. The kiss here suggests love, passion, vulnerability, fear, need, and desire all at once.

The photo of two lesbian lovers, titled simply *Kiss*, taken by Tanya Chalkin, circa 2002, recalls the medieval meaning of the kiss as a subversive act. Unlike the Elvis kiss or the first homosexual kiss on the silver screen, it barely caused a stir when it came out and, in fact, has become popular on posters sold on university campuses. The story of the kiss is, in large part, a side-story of social evolution, not revolution. The fact that Chalkin's photo is now as acceptable as Eisenstaedt's photo of a man kissing a woman passionately indicates that we have indeed become emancipated from the yoke of pseudo-moralism. The kiss appears in the photo as intimate and loving. Both women are mirror images of each other, suggesting a kind of doppelganger theme of a woman embracing her fleshly counterpart. Only the hairstyles are different. Perhaps the photo is successful because it contains a message of true liberation from the past—a message that, as maintained throughout, was stamped into the first kiss, which was both a statement of defiance against rigid courtship and marriage traditions and an act of fervent emotional warmth and spiritual union.

At the 2003 MTV Video Music Awards, Madonna open-mouth kissed Britney Spears. This was not so much important for its shock value, as it was for its establishment of a new system of sexual mores based on an "in-your-face prurience." Another example of a media kiss that was certainly subversive in its effect in the era in which it was performed was the first TV interracial kiss performed on *Star Trek* in 1968, between Captain James T. Kirk (William Shatner) and Lieutenant Uhura (Michelle Nichols) (see figure 4.4).

Figure 4.4 *Captain Kirk Kissing Lieutenant Uhura* (Star Trek, 1968)

This kiss is preceded by touching and rubbing, because the pair is initially trying to resist kissing each other. The reason for the kiss is, actually, because the two are being forced into it by a strange people called the Plutonians who are using tele-kinesis to control the crew of the starship. Forced or not, they did kiss and, clearly, enjoyed it. The kiss went a long way at the time toward breaking down of the artificial barriers between the races.

The TV screen showcased another famous, albeit portentous, kiss in 1981. The balcony kiss between Prince Charles and Lady Diana on July 29, 1981, came to be known as the "fairytale kiss." An estimated global TV audience of 750 million watched it. A closer look at the kiss shows that it has an eerie ominous quality to it—Diana is leaning into Charles's kiss and it looks like she is straining her neck in an attempt to reach him. He looks aloof. Was the future foretold by a kiss, as in fairy tales?

Of all the grand visions conjured up by the human imagination, few captivate us more than the moment when lovers lock in a passionate kiss. When captured in images, these tell us much more than words alone can tell, uniting us all in a profoundly human way, as Kirshenbaum argues:

> In the modern world kissing is extremely popular—perhaps more than at any other time in human history. We celebrate iconic kissing photographs, like the one between a sailor and a nurse captured by Alfred Eisenstaedt in V-J Day in Times Square that appeared in *Life* magazine. We admire artistic kisses, such as Gustav Klimt's painting of the same name. We can't forget unexpected kisses, like that shared by Al and Tipper Gore during the 2000 Democratic National Convention. But that's just the beginning. The MTV Video Music Awards memorably featured Michael Jackson kissing Lisa Marie Presley, and later Madonna kissing Britney Spears and Christina Aguilera. Later Sacha Baron Cohen brought us Borat, a character who manages to kiss nearly everyone he encounters—leaving quite an impression on both recipient and audiences. These moments made headlines around the world with images that will be discussed

for decades—perhaps because they are reminders that celebrities, icons, and leaders are not all different from us. We may vary in skin tone, language and customs, but in regions around the world kissing has become perhaps the single most universal and humanizing practice that we share. [17]

Selling the Kiss

Perhaps no other commercial institution in modern society is as adaptive to trends, and the changing needs of people, than is the advertising one. It is little wonder that the kiss has always played a crucial role in ad campaigns for products related to lovemaking. Advertisers stress not the product, but the benefits that may be expected from its purchase. Indeed, the most effective strategy is not only to keep up with the times but also to adopt trends in it, blending in with emerging lifestyle patterns.

Advertisements related to romance and marriage have been around for a long time. Newspapers in the nineteenth century included marriage proposals and singles announcements, much like what is done today on the Internet. The following ad appeared on March 20, 1870, on the first page of the *New York Herald*:[18]

> Will the lady with dark hair, to whom, while at a window with a friend this (Friday) morning, a card was shown, kindly send her card to the gentleman, whose name her friend knows? He regrets that he is compeled [*sic*] to resort to this method of making the request, but trusts that, under the circumstances, she will excuse and permit him (mentally) to kiss her hand.

Selling products through ads that feature kissing resonate with many meanings. Transgression was the main one in the well-known 1990s ad campaign by the Benetton line of clothing that produced a shock effect because it showed a priest and nun kissing. The kiss recalls its origin in subversion, flying in the face of the canons of tradition. It certainly grabs our attention. Of course, romance might actually be occurring between the two kissers, but to outsiders it conveys vulgarity and tasteless-ness. Interestingly, the ad caused only a minimal stir, indicating that times have truly changed.

The number of ads that show female lips to sell cosmetic and other lifestyle products is immeasurable. Much like pop art, ads like these objectify the anticipated kiss, giving it an autonomous existence. It is this sense of anticipation that lures us to view the lips and to feel the expected kiss in our imagination.

Whether through paintings, sculptures, photos, or ads, the power of the kiss comes out through the power of the image. Because of the accumulation of these images woman-hood has been restored to its place of privilege and respect. Like others, the ancient Greek civilization was founded by a woman, Athena, who sprang full-grown from the forehead of the god Zeus. As his favorite child, Zeus entrusted her with his shield and his principal weapon, the thunderbolt. Athena's temple, the Parthenon, was located in Athens, the city named after her. She wielded enormous power over the world, becoming revered as the goddess of cities, industry, the arts, war, and, wisdom.

The kiss may have brought back the Athenian age. Or maybe it has brought about a new Pygmalion age, as it can be called. We have all kissed the marble statue of woman-hood and she has now entered our lives permanently, as a liberated personage able and willing to express herself openly. This may explain why the mouth-to-mouth kiss has spread through literature, art, and advertising, constituting the fuel behind the advent, rise, and spread of popular culture. The words of Sheril Kirshenbaum on this matter are worth repeating here:

> In the plays of Shakespeare and the novels of Dickens, kissing is a social expectation, and it seems as if everybody does it. We have inherited a legacy of kissing that has been celebrated a legacy of kissing that has been celebrated through art and liter-ature and amplified over time. In Western culture, many of our most memorable literary heroes and heroines pass their time

waiting for a special kiss to take place. Anticipation moves the storyline forward, and the kiss often takes the starring role. It's the happy ending children have come to expect in stories, from *Snow White* to *The Frog Prince*. After all, what would our most celebrated fairy tales be without kissing?[19]

CHAPTER 5

The Kiss in Songs

Oh what lies lurk in kisses.
—Heinrich Heine (1797–1856)

Music brings out the passions of love perhaps like no other art form, as the troubadours and other medieval composers certainly knew. In his *Republic*, Plato equates music with our need for beauty: "Thus much of music, and the ending is appropriate; for what should be the end of music if not the love of beauty?"[1] One of the most passionate, romantic songs of the 1950s that evokes Plato's "love of beauty" is sung by Louis Armstrong (among others). It is called the "Kiss of Fire." The song casts an enormously powerful romantic spell over all those who hear it. Its first line says it all: "I touch your lips and all at once the sparks go flying." In the conclusion, the song tells us, we must surrender to the "kiss of fire."

The song is really an upbeat tempo version of a famous Argentinean tango called *El Choclo*. Reverberating with the fiery, passionate overtones of the tango dance itself, "Kiss of Fire" brings out the power of music to affect us and to move us romantically. Why is such music so compelling? As American educator Lewis Thomas wrote, in his book *The Medusa and the Snail*, perhaps it is because: "Music is the effort we make to explain to ourselves how our brains work. We listen to Bach transfixed because this is listening to a human mind."[2] From the troubadour songs and then the madrigals to the love ballads of early rock and roll and the more romantic lyrics of rap songs, kissing has always found its way into the music of love. It has often been the primary thematic focus in some songs, such as "Kisses Sweeter than Wine" (by Jimmy Rodgers in 1958) and "The Kiss" (the 2007 album by Bikeride). The kiss is celebrated and represented not only in words and visual art, but also in melody and harmony. It may even be the stimulus for many of the songs we instantly recognize as amorous and passionate. A kiss is not just a kiss, as the classic song "As Time Goes By" informs us; it is much more.

The "Canso"

The instant the romantic kiss made its appearance on the scene as a sign of secret love, liberation from aranged courtship, and as a symbol of the tacit power of womanhood, it was incorporated into poetry, as discussed in previous chapters. Most of the love poetry was meant to be sung to the accompaniment of a stringed instrument, such as a lyre. The first true autonomous music genre was the *canso d'amor* (love song) invented by the troubadours—later called *chanson d'amour* in French. In the *canso*, the poet imagines the lady of his heart as the model of virtue, dedicating his life to singing her praises. The *canso* praised physical love alongside romance, standing in direct contrast to traditional Christian moral behavior. It also highlighted the role of the kiss in lovemaking. The *canso* was clearly shaped by, and in turn influenced, the tradition of courtly love and thus many medieval writers, including Dante and Petrarch.[3]

In his *De vulgari eloquentiae (On the languages of common people)*, Dante defined the *canso* as fiction, an early use of that word.[4] This is because the texts of the songs dealt with courtly love, chivalry, and the power of the furtive kiss to change the world. By fiction, Dante was referring to the new world order of lovemaking that was emerging at the time, invented by the poets themselves, rather than received from tradition. Some of the songs were, actually, satirical, revealing that the troubadours were aware of the larger fiction of courtly love as an unattainable goal in practical reality. The earliest troubadour whose songs have survived was Guilhèm de Peitus, known as Duke William IX of Aquitaine (1071–1126). Medievalist Peter Dronke suggests his songs represented the "summit" in the *canso* genre.[5] In total, over 2,500 troubadour songs of love have come down to us, indicating how popular the form and the emerging concept of ideal, but liberated, love had become.[6] The master of the *canso* was, according to music critics, Bernart de Ventadorn, whose works are still kept alive in many conservatories of music today. He was highly regarded by his contemporaries, and his songs became popular throughout the medieval period.[7] They were the first true pop songs of history, since they were written about common people falling in love and attracted a wide resonating response from medieval audiences.

The *cansi* reveal that knighthood and chivalry were popular themes in the medieval imagination of common people. They both recounted and invented stories of kings, knights, and their ladies. The stories revolved around life in castles, acts of chivalry toward noble women, real or fictional, and tournaments and jousts. The *cansi*, also called *chansons de geste*, idealized love among knights and their ladies, married or not. Some troubadours were knights themselves and wrote exaggerated accounts of their own amorous exploits. Many European kings, such as Richard the Lion-Hearted of England and Alfonso X of Castile and Leon, also composed chansons, seeing romantic love as a noble act that, if realized, would ennoble them spiritually.

The troubadours performed mainly their own songs. Others who played them were called jongleurs (performers) and *cantaires* (singers). Some troubadours were both singers and minstrels, carrying love songs from some aristocrat to his lady or mistress as invitations to romance. They were, thus, the precursors of the "singing telegram." Romance had become a business. Troubadours would also work exclusively for a noble patron entertaining the court with their songs. They praised both love and the patron, mocking his enemies in love and war. The minstrels, on the other hand, were storytellers, jugglers, clowns, and tumblers. They were wandering performers who were known by various names in different countries, entertaining the village folk, not the aristocrats. At around the same time in Germany the minstrels had a counterpart in the *Minnesinger*, who sang poetry to the accompaniment of musicians at court festivals. *Minne* was a German word standing for love. The courtly love of the Minnesingers, like that of many troubadours, was typically the hopeless love of a knight for a lady of high station. The songs portrayed the knight's plea and the lack of response by the lady, who usually remained unapproachable. The most famous Minnesinger of the 1200s was Tannhauser, made famous by Richard Wagner in his opera *Tannhauser* (1843). Legend has it that Tannhauser led a restless life, even going to the Holy Land on a crusade. A ballad of the 1500s tells the story that one evening, as he was riding, a beautiful woman appeared before him. He took her to be the goddess Venus, following her to a palace inside a mountain and spending seven years together with her there. Tannhauser then left and went on a pilgrimage to Rome to seek forgiveness for his sins, which was never given to him by the pope. So, he went sorrowfully back to Venus.[8]

The *cansi* were essentially musical settings of poems that were influenced by, or derived from, the tradition known as the *dolce stil nuovo* (sweet new style) in Italy—a tradition that extolled the woman as an *angelo* (angel), essentially putting her on a pedestal and thus resurrecting the Pygmalion myth. The poems were among the first literary works to break away from the use of Latin as the language of writing and to adopt the emerging vernaculars, the languages spoken by the people. The first to use the new style was the so-called Sicilian School that emerged at the court of Emperor Frederick II, who ruled in the city of Palermo during the first half of the 1200s.

Frederick gathered many intellectuals and poets around him and together they came to be known as the Sicilian School, because they wrote in a refined Sicilian dialect. Their poems imitated the love poems of the troubadours, but they also created new forms of poetry, such as the sonnet. When the School ceased to exist with the end of the Sicilian court, in 1226, Sicilian poetry had gained broad popularity, and was widely imitated in other parts of Italy. It was the poet Guido Guinizelli of Bologna who termed the style, *Il dolce stil nuovo*, adding an idealistic spiritual dimension to the troubadour *canso*, whereby women were viewed as angelic creatures and love as the source of all virtue. The kiss in this new poetic framework became the conduit to spiritual love, not a prelude to sex. The idea of the woman as an angel has been inherited by the contemporary pop ballad style, in songs such as Curtis Lee's "Pretty Little Angel Eyes" (1961) and Neil Sedaka's "Next Door to an Angel" (1962). The lyrics of these songs resonate unconsciously with the same celestial metaphors invented by the *dolce stil nuovo*. As Sedaka puts it, he lives "right next door to an angel," and aspires to make that angel his own. This image reverberates with unconscious historical connections to the *Divina Commedia* where Dante meets up with his own angel, Beatrice, in *Il Paradiso* (paradise).

Predictably, in some of the lyrical portraits, the metaphor of the female angel is juxtaposed against that of the female as a devil (femme fatale), as in Elvis Presley's "The Devil in Disguise" (1963) where the interplay between the woman's appearance as angelic and her character as femme fatale comes out perfectly: "You look like an angel," but, as he concludes, "You're the devil in disguise." In the same song, the kiss is portrayed not as a conduit to the woman's angelic soul, but, instead, as a ploy she uses deviously to entrap and ensnare her man. This dual portrait of women is actually an ancient one, found among the symbolic and representational traditions of cultures across the world. On the one side, we find legends of women goddesses and heroines as possessing world-disordering sexual power, noticeable in the stories about Lilith, Delilah, Salome, and Helen of Troy, among many others. On the other, we find myths of women as possessing a world-harmonizing emotional power, noticeable in the stories about Gaia, Eve, and the Madonna. Throughout time and across cultures, women have been viewed, in effect, as having two natures packed into one body—the "mother" and "angel" versus the "femme-fatale" or "succubus." The Bible represents this dualism in the person of Eve (the mother) and Lilith (the femme fatale). Lilith has always been depicted as (sexually) dangerous, disruptive, and rebellious. In the biblical reference to her (Isaiah 34:14), she is characterized as a desert demon. According to another legend, God created Lilith out of earth in the same way that he created the first man. The pair immediately began to quarrel, because Lilith refused to submit to Adam. Lilith fled. God sent three angels to bring her back, who told her that if she refused to return, one of her children would die each day. Lilith refused defiantly and vowed to seek revenge by harming all newborn infants. This dualism was implicit in the *canso*, which not only emphasized the angelic nature of womanhood but also her deceptive nature in the fact that she rarely gave in to the man. This dualism is still around, as pop songs such as the one by Elvis show.

In sum, the *canso* was the first love ballad of music history, as popular in the medieval ages as pop music about love is today. Love and sex, along with secret trysts and the praise of women, were all the rage in the medieval period, and all were connected to the act of kissing, without which they would (literally) make no sense. Though some *cansi* have relatively straightforward rhyme schemes, some are often densely allegorical and highly formulaic, giving them an artificial flavor to the modern ear. The *canso* gave way to the more sophisticated *balada* (Provençal for "song to dance to"), or the ballad, in English, associating the poetry of love and dancing in a more musically-interesting way. A ballad is a song that tells a dramatic story. Most ballads are folk songs or imitations of folk music. Although the "song in dance" has ancient roots, the particular form that it took in the medieval period was vastly different in its overall meaning. The ballad is about the purity and power of romance and sometimes about the foibles of lovers. Often, one person sang the story and dancers joined in on the refrain. During the eighteenth century writers began taking an interest in ballads they had heard sung. Many poets of the Romantic period adopted the ballad form passing it on to poets and songwriters of today.

The Madrigal

A Renaissance offshoot of the *canso* in Italy was the *madrigal*, which continued the tradition of "love in song" started by the troubadours. It is a musical form in which two or more voices sing separate melodies to a literary text, with one voice per part and with or without instrumental accompaniment. The solo singer of the *canso* is the precursor of the contemporary ballad singer, or crooner, while the group of singers of the madrigal are the precursors of the pop groups like the Mills Brothers, the Andrews Sisters, the Platters and the Drifters. The madrigal became equally popular among the nobility and common people, showing that social boundaries were crumbling as popular culture was spreading. Madrigals were performed in piazzas throughout Italy, constituting one of the first examples of open-air music gigs in Europe.[9]

The term madrigal is applied to two kinds of songs. The first, which emerged in the early 1300s, consisted of pastoral love texts, and the second, which became popular in the early 1500s, took on a more serious nature, developing into the classical madrigal that became an early genre of what came to be called classical music. By the early 1600s, the madrigal had become almost obsolete in Europe. But it left its mark on the evolution of popular music, including on contemporary genres known under various names, including the "barbershop quartet" and various other modern-day a capella styles. Content-wise, the lyrics speak of love that is unfulfilled in a way that resembles the "hurtin' music" of country music. The actual madrigal style was revived briefly by Gilbert and Sullivan in their comic opera *The Mikado* (1985) with their song from the musical titled "Brightly Dawns Our Wedding Day" and by the rock group Rush with their song "Madrigal" (1977).

The greatest composer of madrigals was Claudio Monteverdi (1567–1643), whose works greatly influenced the change from the rigid and formulaic style of both the medieval *canso* and the Renaissance madrigal to the emotional style of baroque music, considered the first period of classical music. Monteverdi was also the first important composer of opera. His madrigals are highly emotional and hauntingly beautiful, leading to the bel canto (beautiful song) movement of the subsequent two centuries, which forms the basis of the melodies of modern styles. Bel canto implied a voice that produced a lovely, even level of melody throughout the song. The madrigals and the bel canto songs make kissing the crux of lovemaking. An example of this is the following madrigal written by Luca Marenzio in 1570, one of the most renowned composers of madrigals in his day:

> O merry world when ev'ry lover with his mate,
> Might walk from mead to mead, and cheerfully relate
> Sour pleasures, and sweet griefs, following a wanton state.
> Those days knew no suspect; each one might freely prate,
> And dance and sing and play with his consociate.
> Then lovers used like turtles kiss full lovingly.
> O honey days and customs of antiquity!
> But now the world so full is of fond jealousy,
> The charity we term wanton iniquity.[10]

Although interpreting love songs such as this one is fraught with problems of retrofitting interpretations, the thing to note is the use of lyrics that are virtually the same as the ones used today in pop songs about love, especially in expressing the contrasting nature of love with verbal juxtapositions such as "sour pleasures," "sweet griefs," and "fond jealousy." The culmination of love occurs when the lovers kiss "full lovingly," which evokes unconscious images of "honey days" and "customs of antiquity," alluding to the timelessness of the kiss.

The Aria

The *canso* and the madrigal led to the aria, the vocal solo that expresses the feelings and thoughts of characters in an opera. Opera itself is the genre that prefigures the rise of contemporary popular music, meant to appeal to large audiences. Some arias are written for two or more singers, and often intended to highlight a singer's virtuosic capabilities. In the late nineteenth century, Richard Wagner almost eliminated the aria, wanting to produce a seamless flow of music in his music dramas, so that the voice would be treated like any other instrument. The aria, for Wagner, was too much connected with an ever-emerging popular music style, whereas he wanted to write music for the sake of music and the greater goal of art for its own sake. In his volume titled *Art and Politics*, Wagner shows himself to be deeply annoyed by the rise of a popular music culture, criticizing the Germany of his era as finding entertainment in cheap theater, vulgar songs, and clumsy imitations of foreign art.[11] Citing "music's wonderman" Johann Sebastian Bach as his precursor, Wagner sought to persuade his contemporaries that real music was more than simple melodies and that a culture's destiny was shaped by the level of its music. But Wagner could not stem the tide, nor could he stop lyrical, aria-based, opera from being revived constantly in music halls throughout Europe. Opera has a fanatical following to this day.

Opera became popular and prospered at first in Renaissance Florence, when two Florentine musicians, Giulio Caccini and Jacopo Peri, wrote "Dafne" in 1597. This led to the establishment of the *Camerata,* consisting of a group of noblemen, musicians, and poets who had developed a deep interest in the culture of ancient Greece, especially its drama. They believed that the Greeks sang rather than recited their tragedies. So, they wanted to re-create the spirit of these tragedies with their own new music. At first, they called their compositions *dramma per musica* (drama for music) or *opera in musica* (musical work). The term "opera" comes from the shortened form of the latter. From there, opera spread quickly throughout Italy. The principal Italian opera center up to and including the seventeenth century was Venice. Other important venues were Rome and Naples. In this period a clear differentiation was made between the aria and the recitativo (used for plot information and dialogue). Baroque opera was characterized, above all else, by the use of the aria as a showpiece. The Venetian and Roman audiences loved this new style of song, since it could be sung outside the theater by anyone with a minimal ear for music. Ballet was introduced into the spectacle, not as an intrinsic component of the opera but, typically, as simple diversion between acts or parts.

Throughout the seventeenth century, the Italian aria style, with its emphasis on beautiful melody, had spread to most parts of Europe. The only country where this did not happen was France. There, an Italian-born composer, Jean Baptiste Lully (1632–1687), founded a French school of opera. Lully's patron was Louis XIV. Lully designed his operas to convey the pomp and splendor of the French court. He accomplished this primarily through massive, slow-moving choral and instrumental episodes. Lully also used ballet more prominently than did Italian composers. His libretti were based on classical French tragedies. By the eighteenth century, the so-called classical period of Western music, opera had become a major art form throughout Europe. But, as a consequence, the bulk of operas became rigidly formalized, consisting of little more than a series of spectacular arias based on a predictable formula. Singers were valued more for their beautiful voices and virtuoso singing abilities than for their acting and aesthetic artistry.

Several composers in the eighteenth century tried to change matters, developing other forms of the aria, as well as making greater use of choral and instrumental music. The composer who transformed opera into a truly serious art form was

Wolfgang Amadeus Mozart, who wrote his first opera, *La finta semplice* (1768), at the age of 12. His three Italian-language masterpieces—*Le nozze di Figaro* (1786), *Don Giovanni* (1787), and *Così fan tutte* (1790)—display a genius for musical characterization, and in *Don Giovanni* he created one of the first great Romantic roles—the Don himself. Mozart's German-language *Singspiels* range from the purely comical, in *The Abduction from the Seraglio* (1782), to the highly spiritual, in *The Magic Flute* (1791).

Opera caught on because it dealt with themes that appealed to everyone, not just the cognoscenti and the aristocracy. Above all else, the themes of love, fate, and betrayal permeate operatic texts almost from the start. In the nineteenth century, Paris became the center of grand opera—a lavish combination of stage spectacle, drama, ballet, and music, much of which was written by foreign composers who settled in France—adding significantly to opera's growing popularity. The style reached its apotheosis in the works of such composers as Giacomo Meyerbeer, Hector Berlioz, Charles Gounod and Richard Wagner, the anti-aria composer, who perfected the technique of the leitmotif, a musical theme that identifies a particular personage or idea and that recurs throughout the opera in the orchestra, often illuminating the action psychologically. With his innovations, both in composition and staging, Wagner exerted enormous influence on musicians of all countries. But his new opera style did not lead to the end of bel canto composers such as Verdi, Rossini, and Bellini. They are as popular today as they were in their own day.

Bel canto places primary emphasis on beautiful melody and on smooth, expressive, and often spectacular vocal dynamics. Gioacchino Rossini, who composed famous comic operas such as *Il Barbiere di Siviglia* (1816) and *La Cenerentola* (1817), entrenched bel canto style into opera. The heart of bel canto is the love aria—a song intended to evoke haunting feelings and the rhythms and sounds of pure love, looking back to the *canso* and the whole courtly love tradition. The composer who embodied this style more than anyone else was Giuseppe Verdi. His early masterpieces—*Nabucco* (1842), *Ernani* (1844), *Rigoletto* (1851), *Il Trovatore* (1853), *La Traviata* (1853), *Un Ballo in maschera* (1859), and *La Forza del destino* (1862)— have become staples of the opera repertoire, indicating that people still love to hear melodramatic bel canto songs of love. His *Aida* (1871), with its visual splendor and musical grandiosity, epitomizes what opera is in the mind of most people today.

Opera was defiant of the moral status quo since its beginnings. It included dancing on stage, plots that involved promiscuity and love entanglements of all kinds, in addition to more serious narratives. Kissing was considered immoral and was kept from the operatic stage until the mid-1800s when operas such as *Carmen* (1875), by the French composer Georges Bizet, took on a realistic thrust and included displays of open romance on the stage. This was continued in Italy in the movement known as verismo, from the Italian word for "truth." The two foremost examples of operatic verismo were *Cavalleria rusticana* (1890) by Pietro Mascagni and *Pagliacci* (1892) by Ruggero Leoncavallo. These are short, searing melodramas about love, betrayal, passion, and murder in sunbaked Italian villages; hence they are often put together on the same operatic bill. But the most important *verista*, the true successor to Verdi, was Giacomo Puccini, who composed such widely known and eminently singable operas as *Manon Lescaut* (1893), *La Bohème* (1896), *Tosca* (1900), *Madama Butterfly* (1904), and the unfinished *Turandot* (produced posthumously, 1926). In Puccini, the kiss is more than a simple love gesture, it is an act of heartrending passion, leading to tragedy, recalling various themes from the kiss's history. The same kind of historical allusions can be seen in Czech composer's Bedrich Smetana *The Kiss* (1876), which focuses on the power of the kiss to shape human affairs and human destiny. Based on the novel by Kaorlina Svetlá, the climax of the opera occurs when the two lovers in the opera, who are expected to marry, are left alone and the man tries to kiss the woman. She rebuffs him, refusing to kiss him until they are married. The man leaves her and goes outside to dance, flirt, and kiss the other women of the village brazenly. Enraged and mortified, his betrothed swears to leave home. All is forgiven at the end, as the two lovers finally kiss. The kiss, in the opera, is the protagonist; it is the catalyst behind the actions and the outcomes of people's lives.

The kiss is the force that binds lovers permanently, in life and (more often than not), in death. For example, in Puccini's *Turandot*, in the tenor aria, *Nessun dorma*, Calaf falls in love with the princess Turandot who proclaims that she will be his only through the act of kissing: *Ed il mio bacio scioglierà il silenzio che ti fa mia!* (And my kiss will dissolve the silence that makes you mine!)

In the twentieth century, the influence of jazz and popular American music asserted itself in operatic masterpieces like *Porgy and Bess* (1935) by George Gershwin, *Four Saints in Three Acts* and *The Mother of Us All* (1947) by Virgil Thompson, and *Regina* (1949) by Marc Blitzstein. A twentieth-century opera that, like Smetana's, focuses on the power and transformative symbolism of the kiss is *The Poisoned Kiss* (1929) by English composer Ralph Vaughn Williams. The libretto is based on the short story *The Poison Maid* (1903) by Richard Garnett and *Rappaccini's Daughter* (1844) by Nathaniel Hawthorne. The opera is a romantic comedy, and, redolent of chivalric style, is about the triumph of true love over revenge. It tells of two star-crossed lovers who are separated by the girl's family. The girl became an empress, being forced to marry someone more suited to her station. The boy became a sorcerer, planning revenge on his erstwhile sweetheart since he was not aware of the fact that she was forced to marry someone else. He brings up his own daughter on poisons, so that any boy kissing her would die instantly, scheming that the empresses' own son would one day be that boy. But in the end, the truth comes out, and everyone lives happily ever after. The subtext seems to be that a kiss that goes unrequited can kill someone metaphorically, but it can also restore life to that person when it carries depth of feeling with it.

Today, opera continues to thrive, attracting large audiences. Strangely, people go to the opera not to interact with the singers, to, as they did in the nineteenth century, to sing along, to vent their pleasure or displeasure openly at the performance, and to enjoy it in the same way that we now participate in a rock concert, but to enjoy it as an art form in itself. The functions and social perceptions of opera have clearly changed.

Without opera and its courtly love song predecessors such as the canso, however, there would be no pop music, as we know it today. Many music historians trace the origin of modern pop music to late-eighteenth-century America, when catchy tuneful music was composed by professional musicians for performances in parks in front of large gatherings of people (generally on Sunday afternoons). By the early nineteenth century, opera spread, influencing the development of a soft, mellifluous, sentimental type of singing known as crooning, which became widespread. The growing popularity of this and other emerging popular styles created a flourishing music business centralized in New York City, in an area of lower Manhattan called Tin Pan Alley. The first Tin Pan Alley song to sell one million copies was "After the Ball" (1892) by Charles K. Harris. Tin Pan Alley constitutes the first chapter in pop music history. But, as mentioned, its roots in the madrigal, the aria, the canso, and other previous genres are unmistakable.[12] As Lenny Kaye observes, it was Bing Crosby who took America by storm on CBS radio in 1931 making crooning music an intrinsic part of modern music.[13] With his subtle sex appeal, cool distance, and slicked-down hair, the crooner brought something new to America, as suave and seductive as any European opera star, filled with youthful strength and energy. It introduced a new form of courtly love music to a land made up originally of pioneer settlers. Crooners are still around and as popular as ever.

The performance of opera took an interesting turn in the early 2000s with the advent of *operatic pop*, or *popopera*, a type of song that takes an actual bel canto opera aria and gives it a contemporary twist (beat, orchestration, and so on) or else is modeled after it. It has become highly popular with acts such as Il Divo and Amici Forever, blending contemporary pop with operatic style. In its own peculiar way it revives the *dolce stil nuovo*, emphasizing the role of the kiss as the conduit to an unconscious love that is evoked and brought to life through the act, as can be seen in Il Divo's "Somewhere in My Past" (2012) where he says that only one kiss will let him know that he has known his lover "forever."

The Pop Ballad

The contemporary ballad is about first kisses, sad breakups, heartbreak, betrayal, and passion. The courtly love tradition lives on, clearly, even if current popular music often veers toward the explicit carnality of love. In the background there is always the power of the kiss to bring romance into being, wanted or unwanted. The pop ballad is a clear descendant of the madrigal. As in its predecessor, a close connection exists between the music and the poetic content of the words. From the slow jazz pieces of the Roaring Twenties, to the swing music of the 1930s and 1940s, the rock ballads of the 1950s, the more lyrical hip-hop songs of the 1990s, and the songs of artists such as Alicia Keys and Adele in the 2000s, pop music has always attracted large audiences because it is about themes that matter to people. The best music of the heart, like that of the Platters and the Drifters, is still perceived as magical music (as it was in the courtly love period) that, once heard, never leaves us, haunting us forever.[14]

What constitutes a pop ballad? Like the love songs of the past it has three basic ingredients. First, the lyrics are typically about the power of love to transform people, or in contrast, about how unrequited love can create turmoil and sorrow in us. Many are about how a simple kiss can change lives permanently. Second, the music is mellifluous and harmonious, complementing the lyrics perfectly. Third, it is sung by artists who can communicate the sense of longing or hurt that such music evokes. The great contemporary love ballads, such as "Only You (and You Alone)" by the Platters (1954) and "Save the Last Dance for Me" by the Drifters (1960), have these ingredients. These songs keep on surfacing in movie soundtracks and advertisements. "Only You" was released in July of 1955, becoming an instant hit on the pop charts. It has been recorded and rerecorded with different arrangements many times, one of the most recent being by Diana Ross for her 2007 album, titled appropriately, "I Love You." This is magical music, in the troubadour sense, wherein only love "can make this world seem right," and only the true lover can "fill" the heart meaningfully and, thus, "make a change" in him. The song portrays the loved one as "destiny," and as in the *dolce stil nuovo*, as a "dream come true." The melody is unmistakably in bel canto style. Most of the songs of the Platters are essentially all about love as their titles show: "The Great Pretender" (1955), "The Magic Touch" (1956), "My Prayer" (1956), "My Dream" (1957), "Smoke Gets in Your Eyes" (1958), "Harbor Lights" (1960).

The Drifters came onto the pop music scene at about the same time as the Platters. "Save the Last Dance for Me" is about the ever-present threat of betrayal in love. It was first recorded by both Ben E. King and the Drifters in 1960, reaching number one on the hit parade almost instantly. Like "Only You," it has been resurrected numerous times by other singers, appearing as well in movie soundtracks and television programs. The singer begs his girlfriend to "save the last dance" for him, even if during the dance she might desire to flirt with others. The reason is, of course, that he loves her unconditionally, as in the courtly love tradition, reminding her to remember who is "taking you home." To the sounds of violins and the rhythms of a basic ballad beat, the melody never "lets us go," to quote the song itself.

The power of love ballads is inherited from the history of love as an open process, that is, as something that grows spontaneously in people, not forced upon them by social practices. The kiss has always been the catalyst in this. The words of the following madrigal-style poem by the Renaissance English poet, Robert Herrick, which is a free translation of one of Catullus's kissing poems, says it all:

> Give me a kiss, and to that kiss a score;
> Then to that twenty, add a hundred more;
> A thousand to the hundred; so kiss on,
> To make that thousand up to a million;
> Treble that million, and when that is done,
> Let's kiss afresh, as when we first begun.[15]

The difference today is that the woman, too, can be a troubadour, not just the men, as in the tradition of the operatic aria, where the woman is an active player and poetic communicator of love. Cyndi Lauper's "I'll Kiss You" (1984), for example, has the same frenetic obsession with the kiss as the means of consecrating love as any operatic masterpiece. The kiss will allow her to "corner" her man and never let him go.

The philosophers of Classical Greece believed that music originated with the gods Apollo and Orpheus, and that it mirrored the mathematical laws of harmony that ruled the universe. They also believed that music influenced human thoughts and actions, because each melody possessed an emotional quality that people could experience directly. This may have all started with Pythagoras, as Kitty Ferguson, among others, have argued.[16] While considering why some string lengths produced beautiful sounds and others discordant ones, Pythagoras uncovered the ratios of harmony. Similarly, in some African societies music is considered to be the faculty that sets humans apart from other species. Among some Native American cultures it is thought to have originated as a way for spirits to communicate with human beings. In all societies it is seen as the language of love. Change the beat a bit and you end up with the same musical language of love, romance, and seduction throughout the world.

The kiss has become an obsession, not just a conduit, as Lauper's song implies. We seek it out relentlessly, unafraid of the consequences it may entail. The kiss has become a fixation, perhaps indicating that we probably need romantic love more today than at any other time in history. The following titles of contemporary alone bring out this fixation clearly:

> "A Kiss To Build a Dream On" (Louis Armstrong, 1928)
> "Kisses Sweeter than Wine" (Jimmy Rodgers, 1958)
> "Kiss Me Quick" (Elvis Presley, 1962)
> "Give Him a Great Big Kiss" (Shangrilas, 1965)
> "Hold Me, Thrill Me, Kiss Me" (Mel Carter, 1965)
> "Kiss Me Goodbye" (Petula Clark, 1968)
> "Kisses of Fire" (ABBA, 1970)
> "Sealed with a Kiss" (Gary Lewis and the Playboys, 1972)
> "Give Her a Great Big Kiss" (New York Dolls, 1974)
> "Kiss and Say Goodbye" (Kate and Anna McGarrigle, 1975)
> "Don't Talk, Just Kiss" (Right Said Fred, 1991)
> "Suck My Kiss" (The Red Hot Chili Peppers, 1992)
> "Hold Me, Thrill Me, Kiss Me, Kill Me" (U2, 1995)
> "Haul Off and Kiss Me" (Caroline Aiken, 2005)
> "The Kiss" (Bikeride, 2007)
> "Baby Let Me Kiss You" (King Floyd, 2008).

By and large, pop music genres come and go and are loved primarily by the generation of audiences with whom they were once popular. Among these the love ballads seem to have particular staying power, transcending the eras in which they were composed. Songs like "Only You" or "Save the Last Dance for Me" keep on attracting large audiences to this day. The likely reason for this is, as the troubadours knew, the power of unfettered love to change us. Whatever the style, whether in the medieval period or in online venues today, the music of love continues to have great significance to people, because it speaks to them at many levels.

Theodor Adorno, the famous music philosopher, warned that true musical art can be easily recognized because it moves us beyond the immediacy of the moment in which it was created, whereas, there is little, if anything, in the pop music of the contemporary marketplace that will last.[17] In a similar vein, music critic Greil Marcus states that most contemporary pop music will likely fade away because it "is a combination of good ideas dried up by fads, terrible junk, hideous failings in taste and judgment, gullibility and manipulation, moments of unbelievable clarity and invention, pleasure, fun, vulgarity, excess, novelty and utter enervation."[18] But, somehow, the love ballads survive (in new and ever-changing forms), despite what critics like Adorno believe. Such critics may have forgotten (or at least ignored) that the operas of Verdi and Rossini were intended to be popular and populist. And of course no matter what trend emerges in pop music, it likely will never reach the same aesthetic standards of such composers. This is a moot point, actually, since pop music is not about aesthetic transcendence but of common feelings experienced by everyone. Nonetheless, within the pop music domain, works have emerged that have as much aesthetic force as those indicated by Adorno.

A perusal of the lyrics and current pop ballad musical styles reveals that certain things never seem to change. Romance still dominates and, as we have just discussed, the kiss plays an ever-broadening role in the enactment of romance. The love song remains emotionally powerful and popular as it was in the *canso* era. It is unlikely to disappear from human life, and if it does it implies that such life has mutated drastically for the worse.

CHAPTER 6

The Kiss Goes to the Movies

The kiss of an actress is the most unnerving. How can we tell
if she means it or if she's just practicing?
—Ruth Gordon (1896–1985)

In 1988, a movie about movies and their crucial role in
shaping the modern world, called *Cinema Paradiso* (in Italy
Nuovo Cinema Paradiso), by the then-emerging Italian
director Giuseppe Tornatore, ends with one of the most heart-
wrenching scenes in cinema history. The protagonist, Totò, who
as a boy in the 1950s used to love going to the movie theater of
his village, called Cinema Paradiso, and helping out the projectionist Alfredo is left a package by Alfredo, after his death. He
goes back to the small village of his youth as a famous director, and is welcomed by those who still are alive to remember
him. Totò opens the package when he is back home in Rome
and finds in it all the forbidden kissing scenes that were censored by the kindly and well-meaning parish priest of his childhood. The scene is accompanied by the wistful music of Ennio
Morricone, recalling the kindness of Alfredo and his love for
Totò. The kiss is thus transformed into a nostalgic symbol of a
simpler and more naïve time, now almost forgotten.

Cinema is powerful—perhaps the most powerful art medium
of all time combining sight, sound, and narrative. And the kiss
has always played a role in its evolution. One of the very first
movies ever made, by Thomas Edison, was called appropriately

The Kiss, produced in 1896. It lasts barely 47 seconds simply reenacting a passionate kiss between Broadway actors Mary Irwin and John Rice, based on the last scene of the stage musical *The Widow Jones*. The kiss iself lasts 20 seconds (of the 47). The actors were of retirement age, and continued talking during their smooch. But the movie became the most popular Vitascope (early film technology) movie of the early era of cinema. The subversive symbolism of that kiss, essentially heralding the arrival of the modern world of mass media and mass entertainment culture, while looking back to its origins, was tangible. It caused an uproar, as citizens called for police action wherever it was showed, urging the authorities to charge even those attending with engagement in obscenity. The clever Edison advertised the movie tantalizingly with the following tagline: "They get ready to kiss, begin to kiss, and kiss and kiss and kiss in a way that brings the house down every time."[1] Although looked upon as disgusting, prompting the first demands for censorship in the new medium, the lingering kiss between Mary Irwin and John Rice for Thomas Edison's new invention was a fitting start to cinema (see figure 6.1). The film was a resounding success.

Kissing is so common in the movies today that, as Tornatore certainly knew, movie-making without kissing and romance would be like eating a cake without sugar. The most memorable kisses of modern times come, in fact, from the movies, the medium that has most captured the modern popular imagination. One can legitimately argue that the obsession with kissing today comes from the movies, as the anecdotal evidence strongly suggests. The film *Don Juan* (1926) boasts the greatest number of kisses on-screen, divulging the growing obsession with the kiss among society at large already in the 1920s. The 42-year-old star of the movie, John Barrymore (who portrays the roguish swashbuckler Don Juan de Marana), kissed his two leading ladies, Estelle Taylor (as jealous Lucretia Borgia) and 17-year-old Mary Astor (as innocent and pious Adriana Della Varnese) 127 times in total. He also smooched other female characters

Figure 6.1   From *The Kiss* (1896)

64 times, for a grand total of 191 kisses. The longest screen kiss currently on record lasted a little over six minutes. It occurred between Gregory Smith and Stephanie Sherrin during the end credits of the 2005 movie *Kids in America*. Other long screen kisses include the one in the 1933 Bollywood movie, *Karma*, between Devika Rani and Himanshu Rai, lasting four minutes. Another long kissing scene is found in the 1941 movie, *You're in the Army Now*, between Jane Wyman and Regis Toomey, which lasted three minutes and five seconds. The kiss in Alfred Hitchcock's *Notorious* (1946) between Ingrid Bergman and Cary Grant would have been the longest in history. But the couple had to keep breaking the kiss up into segments to get around the censors, since the movie censorship board of the era had decreed that no screen kiss could last longer than three seconds. So, Hitchcock made sure that their lips never touched for longer than three seconds. In the movie, the two kissers pull back, nuzzle, speak against each other's mouths, kiss again for three seconds and repeat the whole thing.

What makes the kiss unforgettable on-screen is the passion, the circumstances, the buildup, the plot, the unpredictability, the awkwardness of the moment, and often the anticipated eroticism. The kisses performed in movies such as *Gone with the Wind, Casablanca, From Here to Eternity, Breakfast at Tiffany's, Fast Times at Ridgemont High, An Officer and a Gentleman, Witness,* and *Spiderman* constitute a modern-day "kissography," that has installed the kiss as an obsession of sorts that everyone reacts to and visually documented its symbolic power over people. The French director Jean-Luc Godard once wrote that "all you need for a movie is a gun and a girl,"[2] alluding to the fact that sex and violence have always appealed to movie audiences. But then an art form has the capacity to hold up a mirror to the world. As the late Swedish director Ingmar Bergman stated in a 1991 interview in London: "No art passes our conscience in the way film does, and goes directly to our feelings, deep down into the dark rooms of our souls."[3]

Kissing on the silver screen has always intimated a connection to the open expression of the libido. This was brought out in clever fashion by the 1979 remake of *Nosferatu*, released in 1922, itself a filmic version of Bram Stoker's *Dracula*. The remake, titled *Nosferatu the Vampyre*, was by the controversial director Werner Herzog. The tortured, fanged, and pointy-eared Dracula (played by Klaus Kinski) attempts to sexually possess Lucy Harker (played by Isabelle Adjani). He follows her to her room, preceded by his ominous distorted shadow. To her wide-eyed reflection in the mirror he bellows in a dark seductive tone: "You must excuse my rude entrance. I am Count Dracula. Come to me and be my ally. The absence of love is the most abject pain." Being virginal and pure she declines the offer. It is only later that, in true sacrificial style, she offers herself up to him, wearing a white gown. During that scene, we see her lying perfectly still as she awaits his "kiss," and as he gropes her breasts with his long-fingered hand. Then he slowly descends to bite her neck and feed upon her. The eroticism is dangerous and foreboding, keeping us in a state of menacing portentiousness until the rays of the new sun come in through the window, sealing the Count's fate.

As Timothy Knight observes, a kiss scene in a movie is more exciting than any other kind of scene, because we are captivated in a cathartic way by the moment when the lovers finally come together in a passionate embrace. In such larger-than-life images of romantic abandon, all the emotionally stirring elements align, creating a moment of delicious anticipation that "sets our pulses racing."[4] And, as Harris, Sanborn, Scott, Dodds, and Brandenberg found in their 2004 study, that particular kind of scene affects males and females equally.[5] The researchers conducted two autobiographical memory studies designed to assess social experience and memory for watching romantic movies on a date. In both, the subjects selected were primarily middle-class, white, young adults, who were asked to recall the experience of watching the movie they had seen and assess levels of sex-role perceptions. The participants reported with whom they watched the movie, who chose it, and the emotions that it elicited during viewing. Finally, participants were asked to choose the types of scenes in which they and their dates might like to "stand in" for a character in the film. The results indicated that women more often than men selected the romantic movie and liked it more, but, despite common stereotypes, men also reported favorable ratings for romantic movies seen on a date. The women, the study showed, underestimated the men's preference for appearing in scenes of romance.

Early Kissing on Film

Andy Warhol's avant-garde 1963 film, *The Kiss*, as discussed previously, shows nothing but close-ups of couples kissing in unbroken shots. The movie evokes the original Edison short with its obsessive focus on the kiss as an act of sex, love, and human weakness packed all into one. There is no other plot or subplot in either movie. Both zero in on the anatomy, emotion, and power of the kiss. Both are documentaries starring the kiss as the protagonist. Warhol's movie ran for 54 minutes, consisting entirely of a montage of shorter three-minute spliced clips of couples kissing passionately. The gender of some kissers is hard to identify, adding to the subversive symbolism of the act. The film garnered little media attention until much later, becoming a cult classic. Edison's and Warhol's films are an exception. Kissing in movies is, more typically, a part of a romance story. What makes the movie kiss more forceful than its counterpart in novels is that it is literally caught on film for all to see, rather than described in words. And unlike the kiss in paintings or sculptures, we can see it as a performed act. The result is dramatic, influencing us profoundly. Of all the "pipelines" of the kiss conduit, cinema is the one that has played the most crucial role in spreading its symbolism throughout society and the world. Hollywood has taken over from the painter, the sculptor, and the photographer in portraying the kiss's power over all of us. It has brought famous legendary kisses, star-crossed lovers, and cheating lovers to life on the screen. In some ways it has perfected the art of kissing—how it should look, how it should be performed, and even what it means socially and personally. The kiss can be passionate, desperate, tender, sensuous, seductive, enticing, erotic, tempting, funny, ironic, tragic, and subversive; but it is never boring on the silver screen. Scenes of lovers hungering for each other, merging their desires into a kiss, bring the allure and magnetism of the kiss before our eyes, affecting us deeply.

The first movie idols were those who kissed on the screen. Italian-born actor, Rudolph Valentino is considered the archetypal screen lover, worshipped as an idol by female fans of the 1920s. He became so after his kiss scene in Fred Niblo's *The Four Horsemen of the Apocalypse* (1921). Before that he was cast primarily as a slippery, cunning villain. He reached the peak of his popularity with *The Sheik* (1921), which showcased him as a fiery romantic figure. With dark, intense eyes, Valentino was adored by millions of women, who apparently swooned and even fainted in the audience as he performed his kisses on-screen. The kiss in *The Sheik* came to be known as the "tango kiss," since it was performed during an extended tango dance scene in a smoke-filled Argentinean cantina, thus blending romance, passionate dancing, and sensuality. As Emily Leider suggests, Valentino became a modern Adonis not because of his virile appearance, but because of his implicit androgynous sexuality, which became a lightning rod for fiery and contradictory impulses in the early era of cinema.[6] He was reviled in the press for being too effeminate; but at the same time he also brought to the screen the alluring, savage lover who embodied a sexuality based on charm. As the silver screen's first heartthrob, Valentino helped to redefine and broaden American masculinity, ultimately coming to represent a graceful form of manhood that trumped the deeply ingrained status quo of the more brawny and feral male, as portrayed in cowboy and crime movies of the era.

On the female side, Swedish American actor Greta Garbo was Hollywood's first femme fatale, earning this reputation with one of the most sumptuous early screen kisses in *Flesh and the Devil* (1927). John Gilbert was her partner. And the romance on-screen migrated to romance behind the scenes, resulting in real (not simulated) passion in three fiery scenes, and featuring the first horizontal mouth-wide open kiss in early cinema history. Audiences were stunned. The kissing scenes were captured skillfully, with natural lighting. The camera zeroed in on the lips and the sensually seductive expression on Garbo's face. The kisses came across as real; and they were real since she was Gilbert's real-life paramour. For a movie kiss to be effective, there must be the right chemistry between the actors. If it isn't there, then the kiss scene falls flat. If it is, the audience is captivated, no matter how bad the script is. The script in the Garbo movie was dreadful; the kiss, however, imbued it with significance. As David Baird writes, it is often the case that the magical aura that we see on-screen spills over into the real lives of the actors.[7] The effect of a kissing performance captured by the camera, whether it is staged or spontaneous, is overwhelming. Two actors asked to kiss on-screen are really being asked to engage in romance, even if they know it is playacting. The fine line between fiction and reality is eliminated with that movie kiss.

Garbo's other films also dealt with romance in various forms, as might be expected: *The Temptress* (1926), *Grand Hotel* (1932), *Mata Hari* (1932), *Anna Karenina* (1935), *Camille* (1937), and *Ninotchka* (1939). Even though erotic kissing is no longer controversial on-screen, it certainly was in Garbo's era. It brought down many barriers, becoming again an agent for social change in the same way that it did in its medieval origins.

It is relevant to note that the silver screen has often resurrected the Romeo and Juliet theme of medieval and Shakespearean lore, in movies ranging from Franco Zeffirelli's 1968 adaptation to Mark Luhrmann's revisitation in his 1996 *Romeo + Juliet*, in which the sway of the couple's final kiss to defy the world and at the same time to unite them in death is both the climax and the denouement at once. In this rendition of the story, the star-crossed lovers meet at a costume ball, with Juliet (played by Claire Danes) wearing angel wings, and Romeo (played by Leonardo DiCaprio) a knight's armor. They then catch a glimpse of each other through an aquarium tank, standing on opposite sides, and then performing the act of kissing. Kissing occurs throughout the movie. In the climactic double-suicide scene at the end, Romeo kisses his beloved Juliet on a flower-strewn altar lit by two thousand candles. Believing she is dead, he takes a lethal drug just as she regains consciousness. Juliet desperately tries to kiss the poison from his lips, but to no avail. After realizing that Romeo is dead, she kills herself with a gun.

Memorable Film Kisses

A list of the most romantic kisses in film history would be difficult, if not impossible, to compile, because everyone has his or her favorite kiss moment and there is an endless number of kissing scenes in movies that are unforgettable. By memorable here I am referring to things that have had an effect on social history, tapping into the original meaning of the kiss as both a romantic and a liberating act.

Following on the coattails of Edison's iconoclastic *The Kiss* was Frank Powell's 1915 *A Fool There Was* starring Theda Bara (Theodosia Goodman) who was billed as "the vamp." The full-bosomed sex goddess was a sensation, starring in a number of early silent movies. In the movie she plays a sophisticated, predatory female who seduces a feeble and pathetic married man (Victor Benoit) away from his wife and child with passionate kisses. Her line from the movie "Kiss me, my fool" became a cultural cliché that continues to be used to this day. The kiss as a destroyer of a man's reason and its power to lure him away from the safety and shelter of family life, with its promise of excitement and of eternal love, is the subtext of this movie. It is the male's curse.

The kiss plays a different role in *Greed* (1924) by renowned director Erich von Stroheim. The movie is a monumental production that explores the corrupting effects of money and greed on its central characters. The original footage was eventually taken away from Stroheim, cut drastically, and released at a running time that was a fraction of the original version. Although the movie damaged his reputation, because of the prurient sexual allusions in it, it was eventually recognized as one of the greatest films in the early history of motion pictures. The movie features the first "stolen kiss" ever shown on the screen. A quack dentist named McTeague looks lustfully at a beautiful unconscious patient whom he had anesthetized in his dental chair. At first, he holds his urges back, resisting an impulse to molest her, which he had apparently inherited from his degenerate hereditary line. The movie's tagline blurts out: "But below the fine fabric bred of his mother, ran the foul stream of hereditary evil, the taint of generations given through his father." Smelling her hair and perfume, McTeague cannot resist kissing her on the mouth. As he does so, his pet bird becomes agitated in a foreboding fashion hopping around its cage. At the conclusion of the "shameful" kiss, McTeague pulls back, grabs his own hair in distress, and gets back to work. The deranged sexual transgression of that kiss is unmistakable and grabs audiences to this day. The scene is a "mini-essay" on the dangers of the kiss—the force to lead people astray and become engulfed in its vortex of desire and urgency. The word *greed* here refers to the deadly sin that is also a sin of covetousness and cupidity.[8]

A kiss with a French peasant girl during World War I in King Vidor's renowned antiwar movie, *The Big Parade* (1925) is memorable because of the social and psychological nuances it holds, constituting, according to some cinema critics, Hollywood's first true blockbuster.[9] In the throes of war a romantic kiss seems to be the only way out of the conflict. This is Vidor's filmic version of the hippies's slogan "Make love, not war." After sitting down on a bench, American soldier Jim Apperson (John Gilbert) introduces his French peasant girl-friend Mélisande (Renée Adorée) to chewing gum illustrating how to chew it. But she ends up swallowing the gum, timidly refusing his offer of a second piece of gum. Touched by her simplicity, he approaches her lips to kiss her. At first, she resists his advance. However, a little later, under the magical spell of candlelight, Apperson attempts clumsily to say "I love you," from a French phrase book. She smiles and then the inevitable kiss is performed. It is long and delicious, filled with yearning and a sense of doom. However, this one ends happily ever after, as the final scene shows the two kissing and embracing each other at war's end.

Disney's animated masterpiece, *Snow White and the Seven Dwarfs* (1937) reverberates with a whole array of meanings with regard especially to the final kiss, which in some ways recreates the enigmatic life-giving power of the "first kiss," both historically and psychologically. Actually there are two remarkable kissing scenes in the movie—Snow White's tender and affectionate goodbye kiss to each of the dwarfs, as they leave for work, with Dopey coming back more than once, feeling the power of her kiss and, of course, the Prince's gentle kiss of Snow White's cold red lips as a sign of eternal farewell, not knowing that his kiss would reawaken her from her deathlike slumber (see figure 6.2).

This movie has stirred controversy in certain academic circles because of its apparent portrayal of womanhood as passive.[10] But there is a broader narrative unfolding here, that has nothing to do with social roles; it is about the power of womanhood to transform the world and overpower men. The movie has become one of the most popular films in cinematic history, based on, but differing in many ways from, the original 1810 story by the Brothers Grimm. The restorative power of the final kiss is realizable because benevolent fairies removed the curse of death upon Sleeping Beauty, changing it to a deep sleep from which she can be awakened only by love's first kiss. Romantic, climatic, and perfect timing make the kiss memorable. It was not always this way, though. The kiss first appeared in Charles Perrault's 1697 fairy tale *La Belle au Bois Dormant* (The Beauty Asleep in the Woods). In the earliest version of this tale, written by Giambattista Basile in 1634, and called

Figure 6.2   From *Snow White and the Seven Dwarfs* (1937)

Sun, the prince isn't so charming, and is actually a king, who rapes the Sleeping Beauty before leaving the scene.

Some culture theorists view the Disney movie as chauvinistic, since, they claim, it portrays Snow White as passive, awaiting Prince Charming to come along to give her life. Pinsky for instance, claims that movies such as *Snow White* are "archetypal female rescue fantasies with essentially passive fantasies."[11] But, when one probes beneath the textual surface of the Disney narrative, it becomes obvious that the only truly powerful characters in the story are two women—Snow White and the evil queen. The men are either dwarfs serving Snow White faithfully, or else they serve a perfunctory role (such as providing an anonymous kiss at the end). Snow White is a ruler of nature. All respond to her command, from the animals to the dwarfs and even the Prince, who is beckoned to her side by an implicit sense of her feminine power.

Victor Fleming's Oscar-winning 1939 blockbuster *Gone with the Wind*, starring Clark Gable as the rogue Rhett Butler and Vivien Leigh as the cunning southern belle Scarlett O'Hara is one of the most popular American movies ever made. After becoming a civil war widow, Rhett visits Scarlett and looks at her lovingly, imploring her: "Open your eyes and look at me. No, I don't think I will kiss you, although you need kissing badly. That's what's wrong with you. You should be kissed, and often, and by someone who knows how." She resists and this sets us up for the "grand kiss" that occurs when Rhett kisses her fiercely, carrying her up a long flight of stairs to her bedroom, despite her weak perfunctory protests (see figure 6.3). Scarlett's smiling, purring, face when she awakens the morning after betrays how she really felt. Before the era of reality TV, the camerawork in the movie is very realistic, making the kiss scene even more convincing and effective.

Michael Curtiz's iconic 1942 Oscar-winning movie *Casablanca*, starring Humphrey Bogart (as Rick) and Ingrid Bergman (as Ilsa), has a marvelous kiss scene in it. The jazz classic "As Time Goes By," by American composer Herman

Figure 6.3   From *Gone with the Wind* (1939)

Hupfeld, is being played by the pianist Sam in the background. The song contains the memorable line "A kiss is just a kiss." As these words are sung, Rick is pouring a glass of champagne for Ilsa, toasting her with the now famous line: "Here's looking at you, kid." This is followed by an embrace and kiss at an open window, as artillery fire can be heard in the distance signaling the approach of German troops. No greater contrast can be imagined than the one between the kiss and the sound of weapons. The "make love, not war" entreaty resonates powerfully through that kiss. Startled, Ilsa says fittingly, "Was that cannon fire or is it my heart pounding?" "In this crazy world," she goes on, "I love you so much. And I hate this war so much. Oh, it's a crazy world. Anything can happen. If you shouldn't get away, I mean, if something should keep us apart, wherever they put you and wherever I'll be, I want you to know that." She moves closer to Rick's lips, in order to abandon herself in another passionate kiss, ordering Rick: "Kiss me. Kiss me as if it were the last time." As Curtiz's best-known film, *Casablanca* dramatizes the power of love over conflict, and in the movie a kiss is just a kiss in the same way that Gertrude Stein's aphorism portrays a rose as a rose.[12] The essence of some things cannot be explained or theorized. They just are.

Tay Garnett's 1946 movie *The Postman Always Rings Twice* with Lana Turner (Cora) and John Garfield (Frank) contains one of the most unforgettable kissing scenes of all time, as already discussed, given the tragic consequences deriving from the kiss. The two star-crossed lovers are driving along the highway when, at a certain point, Frank begs Cora, who was putting on lipstick, for a long-awaited kiss. Recall here that she responds: "When we get home, Frank, then there'll be kisses, kisses with dreams in them. Kisses that come from life, not death." Frank answers with: "I hope I don't wait." As Cora starts to respond with "Darling," they suddenly stop talking and embrace in a passionate kiss. As they do so, Cora, with an expression of utter terror, shrieks out: "Look out, Frank!" Distracted by the kiss Frank veers off the road, killing Cora. This is a kiss of death. It is, to the best of my knowledge, the first ever car love scene—a scene that evolved into a common one in pop culture. Car romance became a staple of movies about teenagers starting in the 1950s.

Along with *Gone with the Wind*, Fred Zinnemann's Oscar-winning 1953 movie *From Here to Eternity* is considered by many movie buffs as having one of the most famous kissing scenes of all time—a forbidden kiss between Sergeant Warden (Burt Lancaster) and the Captain's adulterous wife Karen Holmes (Deborah Kerr) on a sandy Hawaiian beach with waves splashing on their interlocked bodies. After kissing, Karen says tenderly: "I never knew it could be like this. Nobody ever kissed me the way you do." Warden responds: "Nobody?" "No, nobody," she rejoins. Warden then asks: "Not even one, out of all the men you've been kissed by? Can't you give me a rough estimate?" The clever Karen comes back with a coy repartee: "Not without an adding machine. Do you have your adding machine with you?" The scene quickly degenerates, as his attempt to probe her past was intended to denigrate her character. His knowledge of her promiscuity and previous affairs at other outposts nagged at him and produced feelings of ambivalence about her. But the kiss still sealed his fate. Given the male curse, there is no turning back.

Blake Edwards' *Breakfast at Tiffany's* (1961) has become a cult classic. Its kissing-in-the-rain scene between Holly (Audrey Hepburn) and Paul (George Peppard) is one of the most memorable of all movie kiss moments. The scene starts with Holly on her way in a taxi to the airport to venture on a journey to Brazil. She is accompanied by her upstairs neighbor Paul, who is an idealistic, moonstruck lover. Paul tries to persuade her to stay, professing his love for her: "Holly, I'm in love with you. I love you. You belong to me." She scolds him with: "People don't belong to people. I'm not gonna let anyone put me in a cage." "I don't want to put you in a cage," he replies, "I want to love you." Holly, looks at him tenderly, but counters with: "And my cat here. We're a couple of no-name slobs. We belong to nobody, and nobody belongs to us. We don't even belong to each other." She then asks the cab driver to pull over, to let her cat out of the car into an alleyway, ordering her pet to "Beat it!" A few minutes later, Paul has the cab driver pull over. As he gets out, he cries out: "You know what's wrong with you, Miss whoever-you-are? You're chicken. You've got no guts. You're afraid to stick out your chin and say okay, life's a fact, people do fall in love, people do belong to each other, because that's the only chance anybody's got for real happiness. You call yourself a free spirit, a wild thing, and you're terrified somebody's gonna stick you in a cage. Well baby, you're already in that cage. You built it yourself. And it's not bounded in the west by Tulip, Texas or on the east by Somaliland. It's wherever you go. Because no matter where you run, you just end up running into yourself."

The setting is now perfect for the tension to explode. Paul takes a ring out of his coat pocket, throws it on her lap, and almost bawling says: "Here. I've been carrying this thing around for months. I don't want it anymore." He shuts the cab door and starts on his way. Holly places the ring on her finger. Ecstatic, she exits the cab in the pouring rain running after Paul. When she catches up to him she finds him with her cat who was hiding in a wooden crate; she hugs the cat, placing it in her coat to keep it dry, as the melody of the song "Moon River" plays in the background. She goes up to Paul, embraces him and they kiss passionately yet gently in the pouring rain (see figure 6.4). The movie comes to an end. That kiss, we sense, changes their lives forever after, as all true romantic kisses do.

Planet of the Apes (1968) shows a romantic kiss between a man, astronaut George Taylor (Charlton Heston), and a female

Figure 6.4 From *Breakfast at Tiffany's* (1961)

ape scientist Zira (Kim Hunter), standing next to crashing waves on a beach. Taylor says: "Doctor, I'd like to kiss you goodbye." Zira answers: "All right, but you're so damned ugly!" The remark is ironic, suggesting that the human species may have mutated, rather than evolved, from its ape origins. The kiss thus unites not only two individuals, but also two species in a symbiotic way, thus counteracting the speciesism inherent in humans—the assumption of human superiority leading to the exploitation of animals. The scene caused quite a stir when the movie premiered and may have even been the spark that ignited the debate on speciesism that ensued in the subsequent two decades.

Disney's *Lady and the Tramp* (1945), an earlier movie, was the first to show animals kissing romantically. The kiss did not cause a stir probably because it was an animated film and the scene was so endearing. At an outdoor Italian café, cocker spaniel Lady and mongrel Tramp share a spaghetti dinner, while being serenaded by a waiter. As the two chew on the opposite ends of a spaghetti strand they become startled when they meet in the middle and end up kissing tenderly.

Rob Reiner's 1987 movie *The Princess Bride* is a story-within-a-story. A grandfather (Peter Falk) reads a bedtime fairy tale to his grandson (Fred Savage) who is sick in bed. The movie revolves around that story. Kissing is the highlight in it, as it is in fairy tales generally, of course. At a certain point, the grandfather becomes amused by all the kisses in the story, exclaiming, "They're kissing again." The boy responds: "Is this a kissing book?" pointing indirectly to the magic power of kissing, which is brought out dramatically by the final kiss (in true fairy-tale fashion) between the Princess Bride and her white horseback-riding paramour Westley. At that point, the grandfather concludes the story with: "Since the invention of the kiss there have been five kisses that were rated the most passionate, the most pure. This one left them all behind. The End."

Total Recall (1990) brings this kiss into the age of technology. In the conclusion to the movie (based on a story by Philip K.

Dick), Martian settler Melina gazes at the breathtaking vista, uttering, "I can't believe it. It's like a dream," to which secret agent Douglas Quaid responds: "I just had a terrible thought. What if this is a dream?" Melina counters invitingly: "Well then, kiss me quick before you wake up!" They kiss passionately as the screen fades to a brilliant white blur, hinting that the entire film was indeed a dream. This scene is captivating, not only for its imagery but especially because it is the act of kissing that consummates love, even in dreams and altered states of awareness. Everything may change through technology, but that simple human act will not.

The role of the kiss during the coming-of-age period is explored tenderly in the 1991 movie *My Girl*. In one scene, 11-year-olds Thomas (Macaulay Culkin) and Vada (Anna Chlumsky) are discussing the facts of life, when Vada suddenly asks beseechingly, "Have you ever kissed anyone?" to which Thomas responds, "Like they do on TV?" "Maybe we should, just to see what's the big deal," she suggests. Thomas replies nervously and hesitatingly, "But I don't know how." Vada proposes that they start by kissing each other's arms first and, then, closing their eyes for the real thing on the count of three. The innocence of the act is poignant, coming back to haunt as, later, Thomas dies from a bee sting while searching for Vada's ring in the woods. The kiss is packed with existential meaning, reminding us not only of the vulnerability and brevity of human life, as well as the emotional pain that coming-of-age entails, but the need to live meaningfully day by day guided by love.

One of the most iconic movie kisses of current times is the one that is performed in *Titanic* (1997) between Jack Dawson (Leonardo DiCaprio) and Rose DeWitt Bukater (Kate Winslet) at the prow of the *Titanic* during a golden glowing sunset. It begins with Rose stepping up to the prow to meet up with Jack. He tells her to be quiet, to give him her hand and shut her eyes. He helps her up and then she exclaims: "I'm flying, Jack!" The camera then circles around them, transforming the view of the ship into an eerie underwater grave as they embrace and kiss before they perish.

The *Matrix* (1999) features a sci-fi version of the Sleeping-Beauty or life-restoring kiss of fairy-tale lore, with the gender roles reversed. Near the end of the film, Trinity (Carrie-Anne Moss) revives her dead lover Neo (Keanu Reeves), who had just been shot lifeless, with a kiss. She whispers to him: "Neo, I'm not afraid anymore. The Oracle told me that I would fall in love, and the man that I loved would be The One. So you see, you can't be dead. You can't be because I love you. You hear me? I love you." Neo's vital signs, in fairy-tale fashion, return as she commands him: "Now get up!" whereupon they embrace and kiss passionately.

The 1999 movie *Never Been Kissed* (1999) is a really an entertaining treatise on the art and function of kissing in human life, portraying what a "perfect kiss" should be. The story is about a 25-year-old woman, Josie Geller (Drew Barrymore), who claims to have "never been kissed." Throughout the movie she dissects what she believes to be the perfect kiss, including how the lips should touch, if the eyes should be open or shut, and when a girl should lift her left leg in an L-shape during the act. She is a copy editor for the *Chicago Sun Times* and is assigned to go undercover at a local high school for a story. She falls in love with the handsome English teacher, Sam Coulson (Michael Vartan). But though he is smitten by her, he maintains his distance because she is, after all, his student. In the end they kiss, after he reads the article she wrote about him in the newspaper. The kiss takes place at the end of the movie on a baseball diamond, to the tune of the Beach Boys singing "Don't Worry Baby." The kiss is infectious, as other couples sitting in the stands start embracing and kissing.

The 2005 movie *V for Vendetta* highlights the "masked kiss," a kiss that reverberates with carnivalesque overtones. The leading female character never sees the face of her freedom-fighter lover, code-named V, who wears a mask in the tradition of masked avengers. She is captured, she thinks, by the government as part of a conspiracy. But eventually she discovers that it was actually V who tortured her in order to test her mettle. She eventually realizes why he did it—to liberate her from fear. When she finds out that he is going on a suicide mission to kill the prime minister, she kisses him, not taking off his mask.

Wall-E (2008) is a delightful computer-animated movie. There are two kisses between the two odd-couple characters: the main character Wall-E, the last surviving garbage-compacting robot on Earth, and a sleek white-shelled probe droid-robot called Eve. Their first kiss takes place in outer space after Eve links her helmet to Wall-E's binoculars, causing a spark, and making him float backward in ecstasy. Their second kiss occurs in the conclusion of the movie. A crushed and motionless Wall-E appears to have lost all memory and skills. But he soon remembers who Eve is, after clasping hands and after Eve touches his forehead, causing a spark, and thus igniting recognition. Wall-E comes to life, in fairy-tale fashion, and they kiss lovingly. Their kisses consist of small sparks between them. It is a brilliant metaphor, since even the Sleeping Beauty kiss really was a kind of spiritual "spark" that ignites the soul and gives life everlasting meaning.

The list of memorable kisses could go on and on. The kiss plays a central role in all kinds of movies, from *Rebel Without a Cause* (1955) and *Some Like It Hot* (1959) to *The French Lieutenant's Woman* (1981), *Spider-Man 3*, (2007), *Harry Potter 6* (2009), and *The Vow* (2012). Through the cinematic lens, we have been able to literally see the kiss in action and to get a sense of its power to transform not only the lives of those on the screen, but the lives of everyone.

Controversial Film Kisses

Some screen kisses were so controversial when they were first showcased that they helped, arguably, bring about change in attitudes. The starting point is probably the 1916 comedy

Behind the Screen, which features an early gay scene, even though it was faked. A hired studio worker, played by Charlie Chaplin, can be seen kissing a young girl who is dressed in masculine clothing. She dresses this way in order to find work, so the kisser, a burly foreman called Goliath, believes she is in fact a man. To modern eyes, the scene is humorous, rather than upsetting. But its implications were unsettling to some audiences in that era, who were revolted by the movie, indicating that such activity was best kept "behind the screen," as the movie itself cleverly suggested. The first real homosexual kiss in the movies is considered to be the one that occurred in the 1971 movie *Sunday Bloody Sunday,* a film about a love triangle between two guys and a girl, directed by John Schlesinger. The kiss was performed by Peter Finch and fellow actor Murray Head. The story is about a bisexual designer who is involved romantically with a female (a recruitment consultant) and a male doctor. Not only was the depiction of this "romantic triangle" groundbreaking in itself, but also the kissing between the designer and the doctor was truly a rally symbol. It is no coincidence that the gay rights movement gained ground shortly thereafter in the decade of the 1970s. As it did in its origin, the kiss emerged once again to symbolize both an act of love and social defiance.

The movie actually had a predecessor—the 1927 silent movie *Wings,* in which two male soldiers were seen kissing tenderly. It won Best Picture at the first Academy Awards. When the film was released, no one raised an eyebrow about the scene, mainly because kissing in the trenches was common during World War I. The kiss was a long lingering mouth kiss, between a young handsome soldier John Powell (played by Charles Rogers) and his dying friend David Armstrong (played by Richard Arlen). It was really not a romantic kiss, reverberating more with the desperate love between two dear friends who are about to be separated by death. John actually goes on to marry the "girl next door." But the fact that it was a lingering one placed on the mouth may have unconsciously started the process of opening up America's rigid moral attitudes at the time.

Although homosexual kissing has since been perceived to be just a kiss on the screen, it is still not as common as one would think even in today's tolerant atmosphere. Movies like *Sunday Bloody Sunday* and, more recently, *Brokeback Mountain* (2005), directed by Ang Lee, have continued to break down the biases against displays of emotional and physical intimacy between homosexual men. The latter movie was instrumental in this regard. Nervous ranch-hand Ennis del Mar (Heath Ledger) and rodeo cowboy Jack Twist (Jake Gyllenhaal) grew close while herding sheep in the summer on an isolated Wyoming mountain. Ennis rebuffed Jack's daring attempt to kiss him in a tent, but then returned sheepishly with his hat in hand and accepted their first kiss before their sexual experience. Much later in the film, during their reunion four years later, the two hug each other tightly. Ennis, nervously looking around, forcefully grabs Jack and pushes him into a secluded spot by the stairs where they kiss hungrily, while Ennis's wife Alma (Michelle Williams) accidentally spies on their embracing passion from above and turns away, symbolizing society's turning away as a whole. Things are the way they are, her act seems to be suggesting, no matter what people think.

Three years after *Wings*, the first male-to-male kiss was followed by the first on-screen female-to-female mouth kiss, the center piece of the movie *Morocco* (1930), in which mythic actress Marlene Dietrich made her Hollywood debut. Dietrich looked ravishing, wearing a man's tuxedo and top hat as a performer in a cabaret club. The kissing scene comes early on when, as she sings "Quand l'Amour" (When Love), she moves like a vixen toward the audience, picking a flower from the hair of an attractive young lady while asking her: "May I have this?" She kisses the woman fully and passionately on the mouth to the wild applause of the other audience members. She then tosses the flower she had plucked from her female kisser to an admiring foreign legionnaire, as if to say that, as a male, he has to be satisfied with one of love's symbols, not the real act of love itself—the kiss. The scene caused quite a stir in the media and throughout mainstream America. But the movie nevertheless won several awards including that for Best Director (Joseph von Sternberg).

Another taboo—a romantic kiss with a mentally ill man—was tackled by *Rain Man* (1988). The highlight of the movie is when the autistic protagonist Raymond (Dustin Hoffman) is kissed by the beautiful Susanna (Valeria Golino), an act suggesting that love can rise above any obstacle, social or physical. The relevant scene occurs in a Las Vegas casino elevator. Susanna teaches Raymond how to kiss. She tells him to slightly open his lips, and then she gives him a slow kiss with his eyes shut. Raymond is stunned and intrigued, obviously confused by feelings of romance, affection, and physical desire. When asked how it was, his reaction is as naïve as it is heartbreaking—"Wet!"

Another difficult social theme was confronted by Stanley Kubrick's film *Lolita* (1997)—underage romance. Based on Vladimir Nabokov's highly controversial novel, the movie is about a middle-aged man who becomes obsessed with a 12-year-old girl. The eroticism of pubescence colors the atmosphere of the entire film, giving it a highly charged sexual tension. In one disturbing scene in a hotel, the girl and the man are seen sleeping in the same bed as she French kisses him. During the fade-out, he rationalizes his actions in a voice-over: "Gentlewomen of the jury, I was not even her first lover." Even in today's tolerant climate, the movie shocks and appalls audiences (as did the book). There is no question that the film is unsettling, but it also holds a universal truth—love and romance are not rational; and they transcend social taboos.

Although interracial kissing had become a nonissue already in the 1980s and 1990s, the kiss in the 2001 movie *Save the Last Dance*, still stands out as controversial because it occurs between two teenage lovers. The film won MTV's Movie Awards Best Kiss honors for the kiss between 17-year-old Sarah

Johnson, a white girl, and African American student and rapper Derek Reynolds. Their on-screen romance draws on social issues associated with age, race, and gender. In the end, love conquers all and eliminates such issues through the kiss. The movie ends up being a kind of contemporary West-Side story. It is a testament to the power of love to break down barriers.

A Kiss Is Just a Kiss

In *Casablanca*, as Sam plays "As Time Goes By," the line "A kiss is just a kiss" is played hauntingly. The line is a tautology, implying more than what it seems to say on the surface. The movies have always underscored this fact. A kiss is a sign that is imbued with all kinds of meanings ever since it was introduced to the world in the medieval epoch.

In a scene in *The Illusionist* (2006), Eisenheim, an illusionist, is performing his magical tricks for the King of Austria. He calls out the King's wife, Sophia, who also happens to be his childhood love. When the performance ends, we can easily see his love for her in his body language. That night, Sophia visits him in his cabin to warn him that she has discovered that the king might kill him. Instead of panicking, Eisenheim grabs her and kisses her. They embrace passionately, although desperation colors the scene. That kiss becomes a unifying force, no matter what the consequences may be for both of them. Similarly, in *The Fountain* (2006), Tommy, a doctor, whose wife Izzy is dying of cancer, finds out that she's gotten worse, because she's been losing sensitivity to hot and cold. He prepares a steaming hot bath for her. She pulls him in with her, while he's still clothed, and starts passionately kissing him. It is a desperate kiss, suggesting that love transcends physical time. And in *Slumdog Millionaire* (2008), the main character Jamal spends most of his teen years looking for his lost love. After going on a game show, and winning a million dollars, what he wants to do most with his newfound wealth and fame is reunite with his sweetheart Latika and finally kiss her. The kiss denotes reunion, physical and spiritual. In *Harry Potter 6*

(2009), Harry's first kiss with Ginny after using a magic book and nearly killing someone is memorable. Ginny had helped Harry hide this powerful book in a magic room, where they finally kiss, after years of harboring secret feelings for each other.

But perhaps no other movie has brought out the meanings of the kiss more that *Cinema Paradiso*, mentioned at the start of this chapter. In early scenes we see the village priest signaling for kissing scenes to be removed from films as he previews them before they are shown in town. Much of what was removed would not cause the slightest stir today even in younger audiences. The film uses kissing repeatedly to move the story forward, with Totò saying later as a teenager that he imagined a "Hollywood romance kiss" with his first love Elena. Kissing closes out the film when the grown-up Totò views a reel of film that Alfredo, the movie projectionist, mentor, and substitute father to Totò left for him before he died. The reel is a collage of all the footage that the priest had asked Alfredo to be taken out. It brings tears to Totò's eyes. The reel also contains a shot of Totò and Elena kissing, which he did not know existed. At that point the film reel ends, as does the movie.

CHAPTER 7

The Kiss in the Internet Age

The very essence of romance is uncertainty.
—Oscar Wilde (1854–1900)

Has the kiss changed in today's Internet age? Does kissing have the same kinds of meanings that it did in the past? Will the kiss survive? These questions will be broached briefly in this final chapter, parts of which are based on actual interviews and surveys of young people that I conducted together with various research assistants at the University of Toronto to find out what effects new dating patterns and contexts for meeting romantic partners are having on courtship rituals such as kissing. Will the physical kiss survive in an era when we can send "kiss-o-grams" electronically and when courtship can take various new forms in cyberspace? As Sheril Kirshenbaum indicates, in actual fact, the Internet has made the kiss an obsession worldwide, so much so that, virtually everyone in the global village, now practices osculation even if it was not known in traditional courtship customs.[1] Surveys are consistently showing that romantic trysts now start often through online communications and that online dating has become mainstream. So too has online cheating and betrayal. In other words, today relationships play out as much in social media as they do in the real world,

We live in a new world order, as the 1999 movie the *Matrix* brilliantly argued. People are born into two universes—the real world and the cyber world. Like the main protagonist of that movie, Neo, we now live "on" and "through" the computer screen, and our engagement with reality is largely shaped by that screen, whose technical name is the *matrix*, as the network of circuits that defines computer technology is called. But the same word also means "womb," in its original Latin usage. The movie's transparent subtext is that, with the advent of cyberspace, new generations are now born through two kinds of wombs—biological and technological.

Cyberspace has changed the rules of all the social games we play. It has also brought about a new form of popular culture and a redefinition of what "popular" means. The other side of the matrix consists of the hyperreal world, as the late French philosopher Jean Baudrillard called it, and we seem to be more and more engaged with the hyperreal than with the real.[2] The boundary between the two forms a simulacrum, whereby the two dimensions converge into one and we can no longer distinguish, or want to distinguish, between reality and fantasy. An example Baudrillard used to exemplify this was that of Disney's Fantasyland and Magic Kingdom, which are copies of other fictional worlds. In other words, they are copies of copies and, yet, people appear to experience them as more real than real. They are simulacra that reproduce images to create a new cognitive and social environment for them. Eventually, as people engage constantly with the hyperreal, everything—from politics to art—becomes governed by simulation. Only in such a world is it possible for advertising—the maximum producer of simulacra—to become so persuasive and capable of brainwashing. This is why, according to simulacrum theory, people are easily duped by advertisers to buy even what they do not need. Simply put, they make promises related to life in the hyperreal. It is instructive to note that the producers of *The Matrix* had approached Baudrillard to be a consultant for the movie, which he turned down for some reason. Is the global trend of seeking romance through social media a simulacrum? Is kissing relevant in hyperreal space? Answering such questions requires understanding the connection of kissing to popular culture and how the latter has evolved.

The Kiss and Popular Culture

A main theme of this book has been that kissing and its spread through narratives, paintings, songs, movies, and the like led to the birth and subsequent spread of popular culture. We cannot imagine today any popular representation of romance without the kiss, having become so deeply ingrained in our view of love-making. All this started in medieval Europe, as claimed in this book. The courtly love tradition was the first manifestation of popular writing, loved by people of all classes and walks of life. It also brought about a popular culture of courtship, with its evolving sui generis practices that, to this day, have never quite been formalized, as witnessed by the changing trends in marriage ceremonies, courtship venues, and the like.

Before the advent of the chivalric code for one and all, young women were literally bartered off for marriage. By the Porta Romana, an imposing gate that was part of the outer circle of city walls in Renaissance Florence, there is a strip along the inside wall (the area is now a car park), where one will find an entrance to the top of the Porta Romana. The square below was reserved traditionally as a fairground for peasants in the surrounding countryside. One of the fairs was the *Fiera dei Contratti* (Contracts Fair), when country people from near and far dragged their sons and daughters along to contract marriages. They would haggle over dowries and compel prospective brides to walk up the hill toward the Poggio Imperiale to show off how they swayed their hips. Of course, being more refined, the aristocracy did not participate in this tradition. But they made analogous contracts with other noble families to barter off their children and especially women in marriages that were advantageous to themselves. The kiss changed all that, gradually but surely. It heralded an age of romantic independence, as it can be called, and the writings that emerged from this new sense of freedom were the foundations of popular culture.

Painters, sculptors, songwriters, poets, and others built a whole new world around liberated romance, conditioning people to act and think in new ways with regard to love and marriage. Today we would see something like the Fiera dei Contratti as bizarre and illegal. The kiss changed society and its entire legal and socioeconomic structure. Because of the kiss, there are today many more tolerant attitudes around, leading to an acceptance of the public display of sexuality as a fact of social life. By the 1920s the stage was set for women's liberation, As Linda Scott has aptly observed: "This era [the Roaring Twenties] brought a wave of sensualism, in which legions of young women—particularly though not exclusively those of modest means—asserted themselves by their dress, their dancing, and their romances."[3] Maybe the kiss no longer needs to be a symbol of defiance and transgression; it is something that we can now simply enjoy as an act of romance.

But all this might be changing, as one of the main platforms for the delivery of pop culture is the Internet. Cyberspace has made a "do-it-yourself" culture a practical reality, since anyone can post his or her own work on the Web for anyone else to receive. The definition of pop culture as a culture by the people for the people has taken on a much more literal designation. As Manuel Castells has cogently argued, cyberspace has made it possible for everyone to put themselves on display and to establish their identities in public, and this is altering traditional notions of the Self and human experiences of all kinds (from the sensory to the cognitive and social).[4] The term "global village" was coined by Marshall McLuhan to characterize how people have become reliant on electronic technologies, which have eliminated the limitations of time and space, contracting the globe into a village.[5] McLuhan saw these technologies as extensions of physical, affective, and mental capacities. The Internet is an extension of the central nervous system and has thus heightened our awareness of others. Ironically, this is exactly what once happened in real tribal villages. In the electronic village a form of virtual or hyperreal tribal consciousness has emerged, as human minds from traditionally foreign cultures interact and produce language and art forms that transcend the traditional national borders, leading to a hyperreal mindset that makes it possible to translate any language or code into any other. The spread of the kiss throughout the hyperreal village is a symptom of this consciousness.

But a world united by electronic media creates a hyperstimulated environment that threatens to overwhelm the nervous system itself. In other words, engagement with the Internet leaves us unaware of its effects by rendering them invisible. In an influential study, the anthropologist Arjun Appadurai calls these effects *disjuncture* and *difference*, implying that the flow of capital, images, ideas, and artistic textualities do not unfold in a planned and coordinated fashion, as they did in previous worlds, but crisscross constantly along an unpredictable variety of paths.[6] This leads to a disjuncture in personal and in national identities, with differences being negotiated in new and often conflictual ways.

In the global village the lines separating traditional forms of media have become virtually nonexistent. And while media corporations are still the undisputed leaders in the village, they have become powerless to control all the levers of the cultural flows. Moreover, global audiences are certainly not homogeneous ones. Audiences in such diverse nations as Africa, Japan, India, Turkey, and many others are now unified by the Internet with Hollywood and other main sources of pop culture in the past. Paradoxically, this seems to have made the American form of pop culture even more widespread as such countries adopt it and adapt it to their own simulacra. The kiss however seems to transcend all boundaries and retain its meaning of true romance wherever it is now practiced. In the global village, the kiss remains almost immune to the effects of the hyperreal, as we shall see a little below.

The social media have become integral components of the global village. Facebook (and similar social media sites) is now a major social channel for people to communicate, eclipsing the age of the telephone, changing how we experience social life. Facebook culture is built on the promise of instantaneous connection and of providing a channel for presenting oneself openly to the world. But emerging research in neuroscience is showing that using such media may tap into the same brain areas that make compulsive behaviors addictive, generating the feel-good neurotransmitter dopamine. If this is so, then it corroborates McLuhan's idea that our technological objects are extensions of ourselves rebounding back into us and affecting psychological and emotional changes. As Lori Andrews has recently argued, Facebook has become a huge new brain that may be effacing the sense of individualism and privacy that has been emphasized since at least the Enlightenment.[7]

Maybe pop culture as we have understood it traditionally has run its course. The kiss started it off, but now no longer needs writers, painters, cineastes, and others to communicate its meanings through the traditional realm of popular culture. These meanings are in our collective consciousness, as Durkheim called it (previous chapters). Pop culture has always been appealing because it springs from the people and appeals to them directly, not through the tastes of cognoscenti. It has made personal choice a reality, becoming itself a meta-theory of who we are. But as we change through the matrix so too will the meta-theory. In the global village, everything is in flux. It remains to be seen if pop culture, since its courtly love origins, has truly run its course.

Romance in Cyberspace

Will the kiss survive in an age where we can get anything we want with a click of the computer mouse or a quick touch of the screen or even with a word to some robotic entity in cyberspace? Let's start by considering a website called VirtualKiss.

com with its "e-kissing booth" that seems to have made the cyber-kiss a reality. There are many more like it (even if the indicated website is no longer around at the time this book is published). What is an "e-kiss"? The site reads as follows: "Create a unique e-Kiss™ by choosing the lip shapes, colors, and patterns, or choose from our list of pre-puckered kisses, and send them to someone special." What we really have here is a digital Valentine card. Short of putting one's lips to a screen and osculating with the image of someone on the other side (through some system like Skype), the carnal kiss has not been replaced by an e-kiss. As the e-kissing booth example shows, actually, very little has changed in today's digital world. Cyberspace is just a new textual home for the kiss—like the canso, the kiss sculpture, and other media of the past. The goal of such sites is to get lovers together, to constitute a channel of communication for them, and to make it easier to create love material.[8]

What cyberspace has made possible are, in fact, more opportunities for people to get acquainted romantically. It makes it easier for people to make decisions beforehand as to the suitability of a partner. The real test, however, still comes from the physical contact between two bodies in real space, exchanging glances, kissing, and literally feeling each other out. People are still "turned on" by the romantic kiss, looking for it as a way of making romance meaningful, rather than just perfunctory. Indeed, the research team I assembled for this book asked 46 undergraduate students this very question: "Do you think that romance will disappear if, for example, we can get sexual satisfaction in cyberspace or with robots?" Virtually all of them said no. And when asked if they found that the role of the kiss in romance might be at an end, every single one of them also said emphatically no. So, unlike some social commentators, like Cristina Nehring who, in her 2009 book *A Vindication of Love*, fears that we have lost our sense of true romance in this new age of gadgets and expedient relations, romance seems to be alive and well.[9] Although informal, and certainly not statistically scientific, the survey of the research team is not inconsistent with the research ongoing with regard to romance. One could even claim ostensibly that we have entered a second era of courtly love. In the original era, a man in love with a woman of equally high, or higher, birth had to prove his devotion by heroic deeds and amorous writings. Once the lovers had exchanged pledges and consummated their passion, complete secrecy had to be maintained. Because most noble marriages of the time were little more than business contracts, courtly love was a form of sanctioned escapism. The patterns of courtly lovemaking spread throughout society, turning romance into an art form. The sign of this was that poets and musicians became obsessed with the theme of love. The same obsession can be seen throughout social media sites. Romance, betrayal, sex, and the other themes that made the courtly love literature popular are still there. The language has been updated, but the semantics is the same. The research team checked one hundred Facebook sites and categorized the contents generically of each one into material that was decidedly romantic and that which was not. By using a simple counting technique, the team found that nearly 80 percent of semantic content involved romantic, sexual, and related themes. As the French expression goes, *plus ça change, plus c'est la même chose.*

Studies of Internet romance are revealing that sex and romance are on everybody's mind, almost obsessively. And they seem to be in agreement with Nehring that traditional romance may certainly be mutating in some ways. Online surveys are revealing that people will discuss their fantasies, without actually cheating on a partner, if they remain anonymous. Cybersex is becoming a common online activity, with sites like Second Life playing host to sex fantasies of all kinds. Users begin with chatting about sex, and then move to animated sex. There are now even specially designed genitals that can be used as replacements of real genitals for sexual engagement through specific websites. Users decide how much cyberskin to reveal and which props they want to use. The idea is to allow users to customize their sexual preferences. Scientists are predicting that soon there will be mobile devices that can provide activities leading to orgasms. In 2006, Henrik Christensen of the European Research Network, claimed in the *Sunday Times* that people are going to be having more and more sex with robots than with humans.

But all such scientific musings about the evolution of human sexuality is not new to the Internet Age. Plato discussed all the same kinds of things that the scientists are discussing today in philosophical writings (as did many other philosophers). The scientific slant on sexuality emerged after the publication of the controversial work of Indiana University zoologist Alfred Kinsey, which he began in the late 1930s. The Institute for Sexual Research that he founded in 1947 has often contributed important insights into relationships among human beings, documenting some truly fascinating things about sex and gender that have had significant implications for courtship rituals. While teaching a marriage course, Kinsey realized that scientists had little knowledge about human sexual practices. So, he decided to interview 18,500 men and women about their sexual behaviors, attitudes, and overall practices. These formed the basis of Kinsey's best-selling books, *Sexual Behavior in the Human Male* (1948) and *Sexual Behavior in the Human Female* (1953).[10] The two together came soon after to be known as *The Kinsey Report*. The *Report* was controversial because people saw it as immoral, especially since it portrayed women as highly sexual—a taboo for the society of the era. Even more shocking, Kinsey found that many sex acts thought to be perversions at the time were so common as to be considered almost normal.

But even before Kinsey's work, the scientific study of human sexuality began in the late nineteenth and early twentieth centuries. The German physician Magnus Hirschfeld founded the first sex-research institute in 1919 in Berlin, which still houses an enormous library and myriad materials on sexual topics and continues to provide educational services and medical consultations.[11] Beginning in the early 1930s, American anthropologist Margaret Mead and British anthropologist Bronislaw Malinowski collected data on sexual behavior in various cultures, discovering that although sexual practices were culture specific, they all seemed to share a basic pattern—the need for love.[12] Yet another early researcher, British anthropologist Ernest Crawley, studied the role of kissing in courtship across cultures, finding that the particular form of lip kissing practiced by our society is probably unique—at least in terms of the meanings we ascribe to it.[13] Some things have changed; some have not. The fact that osculation is now widely practiced is not surprising; it is an act that has estrogen built into it, and always had. As such, it can easily be transferred to anyone throughout the earth and in no time "catch on" as a powerful act of bonding.

The Science of Kissing

Betty Everett's 1964 hit, "The Shoop Shoop" song, told us that if someone was in love with us we would know it from the way he (or she) kissed us. Social scientists have become interested in this very aspect of kissing, jumping on board to examine, document, and theorize about kissing. Some of their findings and theories were discussed in the opening chapter. As mentioned, the branch of science that now devotes itself to the kiss is philematology.

There's a lot riding on a kiss, as work in philematology suggests, since the act appears to set off a complex set of chemical reactions that enhance romantic feelings and make physical acts like sexual intercourse much more meaningful. On the other hand, a bad kiss could be the "kiss of death" for a burgeoning romance, setting off mixed neural signals in the brain. In other words, the kiss has a lot of information packed into it. Studies have also shown that kissing promotes bonding, since it produces oxytocin, as we saw. This is a "love" hormone linked to feelings of sexual pleasure and maternal care. Carey Wilson and Wendy Hill studied 15 heterosexual college couples in 2008 between the ages of 18 and 22.[14] The couples were divided into two groups—one set of couples was assigned the task of kissing in a room in the college health center; a second was asked instead to hold hands and talk to each other for 15 minutes. Blood and saliva tests taken after showed that men in the kissing group had a burst of oxytocin, but in women, levels of this hormone fell. So, it seems, paradoxically, that kissing stimulates men more than women. Did the female originators of the kiss know this subconsciously? The researchers cautioned, however, that the non-romantic atmosphere in the health clinic may have had something to do with the findings. Brain-imaging studies have shown that kissing can access any one of three primary brain systems used for mating and reproduction, and it stimulates the production of testosterone. Whichever way one looks at it, the male is the one who gets the most out of kissing.[15] But there is more to the kiss than this. It is not just a strategy in sexual courtship, as we have seen throughout this book.

To assess the question of what a kiss means to the sexes, Susan M. Hughes, Marissa A. Harrison, and Gordon G. Gallup, Jr. asked 1,041 college students a series of questions related to kissing preferences, attitudes, styles, and behaviors.[16] The researchers found that females place more importance on kissing as a mate-assessment tactic than do males, who appear to use kissing to increase the likelihood of having sex. Over 50 percent of the college men surveyed indicated that they would have sex with someone without kissing them, but only 15 percent of the college women answered likewise. The researchers interpreted this in terms of mate assessment, claiming that women place a greater importance on kissing to make more judicious assessments, or to update and monitor the status of their partner's commitment to the romantic relationship, whereas males tend to perceive romantic kissing as a means of gaining sexual access and to possibly monitor the fertility of their mates.

With my student research team, I decided to conduct a related study myself. We interviewed two hundred college students (one hundred men and one hundred women) who were not involved romantically with each other. Although the sample of subjects was much smaller than the study of 1,041 students, we came up with the exact same pattern of findings—namely, over 50 percent of the college males said they would have sex with someone without kissing them, but only 12 percent of the college women answered similarly. However, we also asked a different set of questions that were designed basically to assay what meaning the students placed in the kiss, above and beyond sex. We found that all of them, regardless of their gender, saw the act as a romantic one, often citing movies or songs they had experienced in the recent past as examples of what they meant. Words they used to describe the act included: "spiritual," "soulmate," "divine," "exquisite," "tender," "affectionate," "caring," "loving," "sensitive," and "warm." We also decided to ask them the question that the researchers were seeking to answer: "Do you think that the act of kissing is all about mate selection, at least unconsciously?" One hundred and twelve answered that they saw absolutely no connection to it, often citing animals as the ones who might engage in something similar for copulation purposes. Others thought it could be about mating instincts, but that there would be other ways for the brain to detect such signals. Thus, most saw the kiss as something other than a "mate-assessment mechanism," contrary to what some theorists suggest.

The team also asked a series of questions that were designed to shed light on how young people experience the kiss. When asked about the function of kissing the kinds of answers we received were: "Expressing affection" and "Affirming interest in pursuing a relationship." We then asked them how they felt about their first kiss. The answers included: "embarrassed," "awkward," and "gross." We subsequently asked them what the ideal setting for a first kiss might be. Among the answers were: "while walking together, holding hands," "alone and outdoors," "somewhere quiet and dark," "somewhere romantic, like in a fancy restaurant with romantic music playing in the background." Finally we asked: "What level of intimacy does kissing on the lips indicate (on a scale of 0–10)?" The average we got was around 8. When we asked instead the same question about neck kissing the average went up to around 9.5. In general, these responses confirmed the various ideas bandied about in this book, namely, that the kiss is a symbol of romance and intimacy; that the neck kiss is a lot more powerful; that the setting is one that is conducive to intimacy; and that the first kiss is fraught with anticipation and emotion. So, nothing much has changed since the troubadour days. Kissing is as powerful today, in an age of computers and text messages, as it ever was.

The kiss is also a perfect monitor of love. Either we are "into" it, or it sends out a signal of aloofness and lack of feeling. There is no way to camouflage the message present in a kiss. When we give a halfhearted kiss, we will often get the response "Kiss me as if you mean it," from a disgruntled partner. An unshared kiss is worse than no kiss at all. Many times it signals the end of a relationship. As Betty Everett so aptly phrased it in her classic pop song, "It's in his kiss." It is easier to fake sexual pleasure than it is to fake the kiss. Unlike sex, there is nothing to prove in kissing. Love is either there to be passed on through the kiss, or it is not. The kiss is a perfect lie detector. There is an Italian pop song of the 1950s, titled "Con un bacio piccolissimo" (With a little kiss), sung by a famous singer of the era named Robertino. The opening lyrics give us a wonderful summary of the effects of the first kiss in adolescence (translation mine): "With a little kiss" and with "lips of sugar" "you made me fall in love."

Back to Romeo and Juliet

The story of Romeo and Juliet is, in all likelihood, an idealized recounting of a true historical event. Some place the origin of the real story in the late 1200s or early 1300s. However, it might have been told earlier than that (as discussed previously).

Shakespeare made the story famous. The precise date of Shakespeare's rendition of the story is uncertain. It was published in quarto in 1597. It was Shakespeare's first tragedy, and it is a young person's tragedy, in which the idealism of youth and love are brought face-to-face with hate and death. To the star-crossed lovers, love is both terrible and blissful; through love the two rise to heroism and become truly alive, not just existing, as it were. Their love is a model of what we now consider to be "true love." Such love is melodious and harmonious, like the nocturnes of Chopin, yet imbued with the occasional passionate outbreak, as evoked by Tchaikovsky's *Romeo and Juliet Fantasy-Overture* of 1869, which contains probably the most famous Romeo and Juliet melody of all time, known as the "love theme."

Shakespeare's interpretation of the story is the one that we know best. Thousands of stories have since been written about young lovers whose parents disapproved of their romance. Most of these are now forgotten. But Shakespeare's play remains to this day a classic story of young love, conveying broad human values that are not limited to one place or to one time. This is why his version of the story can be rescripted over and over and constantly updated. It expresses feelings that people anywhere might have at any period of time. Perhaps the most famous of all musical renderings is the ballet by Sergei Prokofiev (1938). Over 20 operas have been composed on the Romeo and Juliet story. The best-known one is by Charles Gounod in 1867. It has been a subject of artists (painters and sculptors) since at least the Renaissance. In modern times, it has been adapted in such versions as a stage musical, *West Side Story* (1957). Dire Strait's "Romeo and Juliet" has become one of their most well-known songs. Obviously, even in a world of cyborgs and love with robots, the legend of star-crossed lovers still holds great appeal—a legend made famous by the final kiss.

In the end, romance is an ideal; it is part of the way we wish to fantasize about the world. Romeo and Juliet were the stars of the world's first great love story. Had they gone on to marry, rather than die in the throes of a kiss, the ideal might have been shattered and the world would have evolved differently. This is not to say that marriage destroys romance; not at all. Let's just say that Romeo and Juliet did not have to argue over who would pick up the kids from a soccer match. The kiss is about the ideal, not the real. But for a moment it suspends the real and makes the world perfect again. The kiss, when it works, shatters the habitual, makes us forget mundane arguments, jealousies, and all the other hassles that make up life within marriages. It is therapeutic as well. This is why couples make up with a kiss. It is a sacred act, warning us that love is not equivalent to sex and that sex is not all that we imagine it to be.

In a relevant work, Donna Freitas found, through extensive research, that university students revile the "hookup culture" on campus.[17] Although sex is common, most students of both genders claim that it is of little value and often rather miserable. Interestingly, she found that among the very disappointed subjects were young men—a finding that goes contrary to stereotypical perceptions of male sexuality. In fact, 39 percent of the men interviewed expressed extreme regret, shame, and frustration with themselves, seeing the casual sex scene as a poor substitute for true relationships. She also found that although most of the interviewees had no idea what a date was, they were intrigued by it and would take it up gladly if it came back into practice, especially dating without sex.

Why we kiss rather than do something else, like touch our ears or rub knees, to express our romantic heart, is not at all clear. Perhaps by touching lips we are in fact breathing our souls into each other. As the twentieth-century American social critic Emma Goldman wrote: "Rather would I have the love songs of romantic ages, rather Don Juan and Madame Venus, rather an elopement by ladder and rope on a moonlight night, followed by the father's curse, mother's moans, and the moral comments of neighbors, than correctness and propriety measured by yardsticks."[18] And, to cite love scientist Sheril

Kirshenbaum one last time, the kiss will survive because it is now completely connected with love:

> And so the kiss persists through time, over generations and among peoples, across latitudes and longitudes. It will continue to motivate lovers, actors, writers, and all of us. For no matter how it began, why we do it, and where it takes place, a kiss often celebrates the greatest emotion of all: love.[19]

Notes

Preface

1. Isadora Duncan, *My Life* (New York: Boni and Liveright, 1927), p. 10.

1 The Popular Origins of the Kiss

1. Joyce Brothers, cited on the website *Life 123* (www.life123.com).
2. For treatments of the kiss in history and its various manifestations, see William Cane, *The Art of Kissing* (New York: St. Martin's Griffin, 1995); Karen Harvey (ed.), *The Kiss in History* (Manchester: Manchester University Press, 2005); Andréa Dmirjian, *Kissing: Everything You've Always Wanted to Know about One of Life's Sweetest Pleasures* (London: Berkley Publishing Group, 2006); and Lana Citron, *A Compendium of Kisses* (New York: Harlequin, 2011).
3. Dan Brown, *The Da Vinci Code* (New York: Doubleday, 2003).
4. Herodotus, *The Histories* (London: Penguin 1996).
5. See Erica Harrison, "Science of Smooching," *Cosmos*, accessed November 2012, http://www.cosmosmagazine.com/node/1464 /full.
6. Leonore Tiefer, "The Kiss," in *Philosophy of Love and Sex*, ed. Suzanne Seney (Toronto: Canadian Scholars' Press, 2010), p. 186.
7. James Joyce, *The Portrait of the Artist as a Young Man* (New York: Viking, 1922), p. 15.
8. Sheril Kirshenbaum, *The Science of Kissing: What Our Lips Are Telling Us* (New York: Grand Central, 2011), p. 40.
9. For a historiography of theories and views on the kiss, see Adrianne Blue, *On Kissing: From the Metaphysical to the Erotic* (London: Victor Gollancz, 1996).

10. Nicholas Perella, *The Kiss Sacred and Profane: An Interpretive History of Kiss Symbolism and Related Religio-Erotic Themes* (Berkeley: University of California Press, 1969), p. 15.
11. Kirshenbaum, *The Science of Kissing*, p. 41.
12. Ibid., pp. 41–42.
13. Ibid., p. 47.
14. Jennifer Wright Knust, *Unprotected Texts: The Bible's Surprising Contradictions about Sex and Desire* (New York: HarperOne, 2011).
15. Michael Coogan, *God and Sex: What the Bible Really Says* (New York: Twelve, 2010). Actually, the amount of writing on sex in the Bible has witnessed a veritable explosion, indicating, perhaps, that in a secular world, sacred texts need to be approached with a different hermeneutic lens. In addition to the books by Knust and Coogan, one can mention the following: Edward Ackerley, *The X-Rated Bible: An Irreverent Survey of Sex in Scripture* (New York: Feral House, 1999); Philo Telos, *Divine Sex: Liberating Sex from Religious Tradition* (New York: Trafford, 2006); Teresa Hornsby, *Sex Texts from the Bible: Selections Annotated & Explained* (New York: Skylight Paths); and Darrel Ray, *Sex & God: How Religion Distorts Sexuality* (New York: IPC Press, 2012).
16. Brown, *The Da Vinci Code.*
17. On this passage, see Craig A. Evans, *Fabricating Jesus: How Modern Scholars Distort the Gospels* (Downers Grove, IL: IVP Books, 2008), p. 94.
18. Catullus, *The Poems* (London: Macmillan, 1973).
19. In Maurice Balme and James Morewood, *Oxford Latin Reader* (Oxford: Oxford University Press, 1997).
20. Lucretius, *De rerum natura* (New York: Loeb Classical Library, 1975).
21. Ovid, *Ars Amatoria* (New York: Kessinger, 2004).
22. Kirshenbaum, *The Science of Kissing*, p. 58
23. Ibid., p. 59.
24. James Jones, *From Here to Eternity* (New York: Scribner, 1951), p. 244.
25. Kirshenbaum, *The Science of Kissing*, p. 122.
26. Andreas Capellanus, *The Art of Courtly Love*, trans. John Jay Perry (New York: Columbia University Press, 1941).
27. Susie O'Brien and Imre Szeman, *Popular Culture: A User's Guide* (Toronto: Thomson, 2004), p. 7.
28. See Olin H. Moore, "The Origins of the Legend of Romeo and Juliet in Italy," *Speculum* 5 (1930): 264–277.

29. William Shakespeare, *Romeo and Juliet* (New York, Random House, 2009), Act 5, Scene 3.
30. Peter Abelard, *The Story of My Misfortunes*, trans. Henry Adams Bellows (St. Paul, MN: Thomas A. Boyd, 1922).
31. Collections of such facts abound. See, for example, Christopher Nyrop, *The Kiss and Its History* (London: Sands and Company, 1901); Cane, *The Art of Kissing*; and Blue, *On Kissing*.
32. Harvey, *The Kiss in History*, p. 189.
33. Giovanni Pico della Mirandola, *Commentary on a Love Song of Girolamo Benivieni* (Baltimore: John Hopkins University Press, 1967), p. 126.
34. Umar Ibn Muhammad el-Nefzawi, *The Perfumed Garden* (New York: Kessinger, 2005).
35. Perella, *The Kiss Sacred and Profane*, p. 243.
36. Willem Frijhoff, "The Kiss Sacred and Profane: Reflections on a Cross-Cultural Confrontation," in *A Cultural History of Gesture*, ed. Jan Bremmer and Herman Roodenberg (Ithaca: Cornell University Press, 1992), p. 222.
37. Kirshenbaum, *The Science of Kissing*, pp. 127–128.
38. For a comprehensive treatment of the "science of kissing," see ibid.
39. Kirshenbaum, *The Science of Kissing*, pp. 17–18.
40. Perella, *The Kiss Sacred and Profane*.
41. Sigmund Freud, *The Psychopathology of Everyday Life* (London: Macmillan, 1919), p. 169 and Sigmund Freud, *Introductory Lectures on Psychoanalysis* (New York: Norton, 1977), p. 365.
42. Sigmund Freud, *On Sexuality* (London: Penguin, 1956).
43. Blue, *On Kissing*, p. 12.
44. Jane Goodall, *In the Shadow of Man* (Boston: Houghton Mifflin, 1971), p. 12.
45. References to such primate behavior can be found in Charles Darwin, *The Origin of Species* (New York: Collier, 1858) and Charles Darwin, *The Descent of Man* (New York: Modern Library, 1871).
46. Michael Sims, *Adam's Navel: A Natural and Cultural History of the Human Form* (London: Penguin, 2003), p. 122.
47. Morris's ideas can be found in several of his books, including *The Naked Ape: A Zoologist's Study of the Human Animal* (New York: Bantam, 1967); *Intimate Behavior* (New York: Kodansha Globe, 1997); and *The Naked Woman: A Study of the Female Body* (New York: Thomas Dunne Books, 2005).
48. Randy Thornhill and Steven Gangestead, "Facial Attractiveness," *Trends in Cognitive Sciences* 3 (1999): 452–460 and Randy Thornhill and Karl Grammer, "The Body and Face of Woman: One Ornament

that Signals Quality?" *Evolution and Human Behavior* 20 (1999): 105–120.

49. Kirshenbaum, *The Science of Kissing*, p. 3.
50. Ibid., p. 20.
51. Jakob von Uexküll, *Umwelt und Innenwelt der Tierre* (Berlin: Springer, 1909).
52. Sims, *Adam's Navel.*
53. Helen Fisher, *Why Him? Why Her? Finding Real Love by Understanding Your Personality Type* (New York: Macmillan, 2009).
54. Cited on the website *PositiveMed* (positivemed.com/happy-life/quotes).
55. Kirshenbaum, *The Science of Kissing*, p. 209.
56. From George Economou (ed.), *Proensa: An Anthology of Troubadour Poetry* (St. Paul, MN: Paragon House, 1986).
57. Guillaume de Lorrie and Jean de Meun, *The Romance of the Rose*, trans. Frances Hogan (Oxford: Oxford University Press, 1999).
58. Marcel Danesi, *X-Rated! The Power of Mythic Symbolism in Popular Culture* (New York: Palgrave Macmillan, 2009).

2 The Kiss in Symbol, Ritual, and Myth

1. Yuri Lotman, *Universe of the Mind: A Semiotic Theory of Culture* (Bloomington: Indiana University Press, 1991).
2. Thomas A. Sebeok and Marcel Danesi, *The Forms of Meaning: Modeling Systems Theory and Semiotics* (Berlin: Mouton de Gruyter, 2000), call these forms appropriately *metaforms.*
3. An in-depth discussion of the history of sweets is the one by Tim Richardson, *Sweets: A History of Candy* (New York: Bloomsbury, 2002).
4. As in the previous chapter, many of the facts on file cited here come from various sources, including William Cane, *The Art of Kissing* (New York: St. Martin's Griffin, 1995); Karen Harvey, *The Kiss in History* (Manchester: Manchester University Press, 2005); Andréa Dmirjian, *Kissing: Everything You Wanted to Know about One of Life's Sweetest Pleasures* (London: Penguin, 2006); and Lana Citron, *A Compendium of Kisses: Facts, Quotes and Curiosities* (New York: Harlequin, 2010).
5. See Richardson, *Sweets.*
6. Ibid.
7. Geoffrey Chaucer, *The Parliament of Fowls* (Ten Speed: Kindle edition, 2012) See also Clyde R. Bulla, *The Story of Valentine's Day* (New York: HarperCollins, 1999).

8. Charles Dickens, *Bleak House* (London: Chapman and Hall, 1868), p. 249.

9. Various accounts and discussions of the origins of Valentine's can be found in Nancy J. Skarmess and Stacy Venturi-Pickett, *The Story of Valentine's Day* (Nashville: Ideals Publications, 1999); Bulla, *The Story of Valentine's Day*; and Natalie M. Rosinsky, *Valentine's Day* (Minneapolis: Compass Point Books, 2003).

10. Joanne Harris, *Chocolat* (New York: Doubleday, 2009).

11. Umberto Eco, *The Name of the Rose* (New York: Harcourt, 1983).

12. Guillaume de Lorrie and Jean de Meun, *The Romance of the Rose*, trans. Frances Hogan (Oxford: Oxford University Press, 1999).

13. Marilyn Yalom, *How the French Invented Love* (New York: HarperCollins, 2012).

14. See Annette Stott, "Floral Femininity: A Pictorial Definition," *American Art* 6 (1992): 60–77.

15. See Sheril Kirshenbaum, *The Science of Kissing: What Our Lips Are Telling Us* (New York: Grand Central, 2011), pp. 12–14.

16. Ibid., p. 13.

17. Diane Ackerman, *Natural History of the Senses* (New York: Vintage, 1991), p. 145.

18. See James B. Twitchell, *Twenty Ads that Shook the World* (New York: Crown, 2000).

19. See, for example, Ingemar Nordgren, *The Well Spring of the Goths: About the Gothic Peoples in the Nordic Countries and on the Continent* (Lincoln, NE: iUniverse, 2004), pp. 191–193.

20. For a discussion of the origins and meanings of love knots, see Charlotte Bingham, *The Love Knot* (London: Random House, 2000).

21. See Jules Cashford, *The Moon: Myth and Image* (London: Cassell, 2002).

22. Claude Lévi-Strauss, *Myth and Meaning: Cracking the Code of Culture* (Toronto: University of Toronto Press, 1978).

23. A discussion of various marriage rituals throughout time can be found in Ethel Lucy Urlin, *A Short History of Marriage: Marriage Rites, Customs, and Folklore in Many Countries and All Ages* (State Park: Pennsylvania State University, 1990) and George P. Monger, *Marriage Customs of the World: From Henna to Honeymoons* (Santa Barbara: ABC-CLIO, 2004).

24. Discussions of the legends attached to the mistletoe kiss can be found in Betty Neels, *The Mistletoe Kiss* (New York: Harlequin, 1998).

25. Cited in Kirshenbaum, *The Science of Kissing*, p. 48.

26. Chaucer, *Parliament of Fowls*, p. 23.
27. For theories about the origins of the Valentine's card, see Robert Brenner, *Valentine Treasury: A Century of Valentine Cards* (Atglen, PA: Schiffer Publishing Company, 1999).
28. See on this point various writings in Michael Allen and Valery Rees, *Marsilio Ficino: His Theology, His Philosophy, His Legacy* (Leiden: Brill, 2002).
29. Found on the magazine's website: http://www.cosmopolitan.com/sex-love/tips-moves/four-kisses-must-master.
30. A good discussion of the Dracula myth in the modern world is the one by Matthew Beresford, *From Demons to Dracula: The Creation of the Modern Vampire Myth* (Chicago: University of Chicago Press, 2009).
31. See Linda Sonntag, *Seduction through the Ages* (London: Octopus, 2001), pp. 120–124.
32. Ibid., p. 123.
33. A good collection of studies on the *Twilight* phenomenon is the one edited by Giselle Liza Anatol, *Bringing Light to Twilight* (New York: Palgrave Macmillan, 2011).
34. Gregory L. Reece, *Creature of the Night* (London: I. B. Tauris, 2012), p. 95.
35. See Montague Summers, *The Werewolf in Lore and Legend* (Minneola, NY: Dover, 1933).
36. See Bruno Bettelheim, *The Uses of Enchantment: The Meaning and Importance of Fairy Tales* (New York: Vintage 1989).
37. See Urlin, *A Short History of Marriage*.
38. Sigmund Freud, *Civilization and Its Discontents* (New York: W. W. Norton, 1961).
39. Carl Jung, *Aspects of the Feminine* (Princeton: Princeton University Press, 1982), p. 65.
40. Willem Frijhoff, "The Kiss Sacred and Profane: Reflections on a Cross-Cultural Confrontation," in *A Cultural History of Gesture*, ed. Jan Bremmer and Herman Roodenberg (Ithaca: Cornell University Press, 1992), p. 230.
41. Émile Durkheim, *The Elementary Forms of Religious Life* (New York: Collier, 1912), p. 12.
42. Georges Bataille, *L'erotisme* (Paris: Gallimard, 1957).
43. Christopher Nyrop and William Frederick Harvey, *The Kiss and Its History* (London: Sands and Company, 1901).
44. Kirshenbaum, *The Science of Kissing*, p. 49.
45. Cited in ibid., p. 52.

3 The Kiss in Stories, Real and Fictional

1. For a historical account of the Valentine card, see Ernest Dudley Chase, *The Romance of Greeting Cards* (Boston: Rust Craft, 1956).
2. E. E. Cummings, *Complete Poems, 1904–1962* (New York: Liveright, 1991), pp. 13–14.
3. Guillaume IX, "Farai chansoneta nueva," in *Les Chansons de Guillaume IX*, ed. A. Jeanroy (Paris: Champion, 1927), p. 20.
4. Bernart Marti, "Amar dei," *Les poesies de Bernart Marti*, ed. E. Hoepffner (Paris: Champion, 1929), p. 3.
5. Dante Alighieri, *Vita Nuova*, trans. Andrew Frisardi (Evanston: Northwestern University Press, 2012).
6. Dante Alighieri, *La Divina Commedia*, trans. Charles S. Singleton and C. H. Grandgent (Cambridge: Harvard University Press, 1933).
7. A good account of the role of Jezebel in the popular imagination is the one by Lesley Hazleton, *Jezebel: The Untold Story of the Bible's Harlot Queen* (New York: Doubleday, 2009).
8. Giacomo Casanova, *The Story of My Life* (Harmondsworth: Penguin, 2001).
9. Carl G. Jung, *Memories, Dreams, Reflections* (New York: Random House, 1963).
10. See Lucy Huskinson (ed.), *Dreaming the Myth Onwards: New Directions of Jungian Therapy and Thought* (London: Routledge, 2008).
11. For a discussion of the Samson and Delilah story form a modernist perspective, see Ginger Garrett, *Desired: The Untold Story of Samson and Delilah* (Colorado Springs: David C. Cook, 2011).
12. Geoffrey of Monmouth, *The History of the Kinds of England,* trans. Lewis Thorpe (London: Penguin, 1966).
13. Chrétien de Troyes, *Arthurian Romances* (Rockville, MD: Wildside Press, 2008).
14. Ibid., p. 34.
15. Andrea Hopkins, *The Book of Courtly Love: The Passionate Code of the Troubadours* (San Francisco: HarperSanFrancisco, 1994).
16. Stanley Wells, *Looking for Sex in Shakespeare* (Cambridge: Cambridge University Press, 2004).
17. Dante Alighieri, *The Divine Comedy* (Harmondsworth: Penguin, 2003), p. 43.
18. Daniel Boorstin, *The Image* (New York: Vintage, 1961).

19. Good treatments of the celebrity phenomenon can be found in Leo Braudy, *The Frenzy of Renown: Fame and Its History* (New York: Vintage, 1997); P. David Marshall, *Celebrity and Power: Fame in Contemporary Culture* (Minneapolis: University of Minnesota Press, 1997); Graeme Turner, *Understanding Celebrity* (London: Sage Publications, 2004); and Ellis Cashmore, *Celebrity Culture* (London: Routledge, 2006).

20. Jeff Guinn, *Go Down Together: The True, Untold Story of Bonnie and Clyde* (New York: Simon and Schuster, 2009), p. 6

21. In Evangeline Bruce, *Napoleon and Josephine: An Improbable Marriage* (New York: Scribner, 1995).

22. *Ladies' Home Journal*, 2006, vol. 46, p. 6.

23. Jean Baudrillard, *Simulations* (New York: Semiotexte, 1983).

24. See Barbara Becker-Cantarino, *Daniel Heinsius* (Woodbridge, CT: Twayne Publishers, 1978).

25. Richard J. Bowring, *Murasaki Shikibu: The Tale of Genji* (Cambridge: Cambridge University Press, 1988).

26. Emily Bronte, *Wuthering Heights* (London: Thomas Cautley Newby, 1847).

27. E. L. James, *Fifty Shades of Grey* (New York: Vintage, 2012).

28. Janice A. Radway, *Reading the Romance: Women, Patriarchy, and Popular Literature*, 2nd ed. (Chapell Hill: University of North Carolina Press, 1991).

29. Charles Perrault, *The Complete Fairy Tales of Charles Perrault*, trans. Nicoletta Simborowski and Neil Phillip (New York: Clarion Books, 1993).

30. James B. Twitchell, *Twenty Ads that Shook the World* (New York: Crown, 2000).

31. Karen Harvey, *The Kiss in History* (Manchester: Manchester University Press, 2005).

32. Sigmund Freud, *On Sexuality* (Harmondsworth: Penguin, 1956).

4   The Kiss in Images

1. Ovid, *Metamorphoses*, trans. A. D. Melville (Oxford: Oxford University Press, 2009).

2. George Bernard Shaw, *Pygmalion* (London: Penguin, 2013).

3. The aesthetic power of this painting is discussed insightfully by Susanna Partsch, *Klimt: Life and Work* (New York: Prestel, 1994).

4. Denis Dutton, *The Art Instinct: Beauty, Pleasure, and Human Evolution* (London: Bloomsbury, 2009).

5. Carlo Falciani and Antonio Natali, *Bronzino: Painter and Poet of the Court of the Medici* (Florence: Mandragora, 2010).

6. Alastair Laing, *François Boucher, 1703–1770* (New York: Harry N. Abrams, 1986).

7. Robert Rosenblum, *Master of Art: Ingres* (New York: Harry N. Abrams, 1990).

8. The ambiguity of the meanings of the Paola and Francesca story are discussed by Renato Poggioli, "Tragedy or Romance? A Reading of the Paolo and Francesca Episode in Dante's *Inferno*," *Publications of the Modern Language association of America* 72 (1957): 313–358.

9. Laurence Des Cars, *Jean-Leon Gerome* (New York: Skira, 2010).

10. Paula James, *The Legacy of Ovid's Pygmalion Myth on Screen: In Pursuit of the Perfect Woman* (London: Continuum Press, 2011).

11. Sue Prideaux, *Edvard Munch: Behind the Scream* (New Haven: Yale University Press, 2007).

12. See Mike Venezia, *Roy Lichtenstein* (New York: Children's Press, 2002) and James Rondeau and Sheena Wagstaff, *Roy Lichtenstein: A Retrospective* (Chicago: Art Institute of Chicago, 2012).

13. Cited in David Wallechinsky and Amy Wallace, *The Book of Lists* (Edinburgh: Canongate Books, 2004), p. 22.

14. Insightful treatments of Rodin's work can be found in Yvonne Taillandier, *Rodin* (New York: Crown, 1977); Catharine Lampert, *Rodin: Sculpture and Drawings* (New Haven: Yale University Press, 1986); and Rainer Crone and Siegfried Salzmann (eds.), *Rodin: Eros and Creativity* (Munich: Prestel, 1992).

15. A good discussion of Brancusi's art is the one by Eric Shanes, *Constantin Brancusi* (New York: Abbeville Publishing, 1989).

16. Alfred Eisenstaedt, *Eisenstaedt on Eisenstaedt: A Self-Portrait* (New York: Abbeville Press, 1985).

17. Sheril Kirshenbaum, *The Science of Kissing: What Our Lips Are Telling Us* (New York: Grand Central, 2011), pp. 66–67.

18. Cited in ibid., p. 192.

19. Kirshenbaum, *The Science of Kissing*, pp. 59–60.

5   The Kiss in Songs

1. Plato, *The Republic* (New York: Sphere Books, 1986), p. 171.

2. Lewis Thomas, *The Medusa and the Snail: More Notes of a Biology Watcher* (London: Penguin, 1979), p. 87.

3. For a comprehensive treatment of troubadour songs and poetry, see Simon Gaunt and Sarah Kay (eds.), *The Troubadours: An*

Introduction (Cambridge: Cambridge University Press, 1999) and Elizabeth Audrey, *The Music of the Troubadours* (Bloomington: Indiana University Press, 2000).

4. Dante Alighieri, *De vulgari eloquentia*, ed. Steven Botteril (Cambridge: Cambridge University Press, 2005).

5. Peter Dronke, *The Medieval Lyric* (Woodbridge: Boydell & Brewer, 1996), p. 111.

6. F. R. P. Akehurst and Judith M. Davis (eds.), *A Handbook of the Troubadours* (Berkeley: University of California Press, 1995), p. 23.

7. Works treating the history and importance of the troubadours to music and poetry include Frederick Morris Warren, "The Troubadour 'Canso' and Latin Lyric Poetry," *Modern Philology* 9 (1912): 469–487; H. J. Chayton, *The Troubadours* (Cambridge: Cambridge University press, 1912); Roger Boase, *The Origin and Meaning of Courtly Love* (Manchester: Manchester University Press, 1977); and Gaunt and Kay, *The Troubadours*.

8. A comprehensive collection and analysis of the music of the Minnesingers is the one by Ronald J. Taylor, *The Art of the Minnesinger: Songs of the Thirteenth Century* (Cardiff: University of Wales Press, 1968).

9. Comprehensive treatments of the madrigal can be found in Alfred Einstein, *The Italian Madrigal* (Princeton: Princeton University Press, 1949) and Iain Fenlon and James Haar, *The Italian Madrigal in the 16th Century: Sources and Interpretation* (Cambridge: Cambridge University Press, 1988).

10. In Thomas Oliphant, *La musa madrigalesca* (London: Calkin and Budd, 1837), p. 60. For a study of Marenzio's music, see James Chatter, *Luca Marenzio and the Italian Madrigal, 1577–1593* (Ann Arbor: University of Michigan Press, 1981).

11. Richard Wagner, *Art and Politics*, trans. William A. Ellis (Lincoln: University of Nebraska Press, 1995).

12. The role of Tin Pan Alley in the evolution of popular music is discussed by Isaac Goldberg, *Tin Pan Alley: A Chronicle of American Music* (New York: Frederick Ungar, 1930); David A. Jasen, *Tin Pan Alley: The Composers, the Songs, the Performers and Their Times* (New York: Primus, 1988); and Nicholas E. Tawa, *The Way to Tin Pan Alley: American Popular Song, 1866–1910* (New York: Schirmer Books, 1990).

13. Lenny Kaye, *You Call It Madness: The Sensuous Song of the Croon* (New York: Villiard, 2004).

14. Good treatments of the rise and importance of popular to the constitution of popular culture include Ted Greenwald, *Rock & Roll* (New York: Friedman, 1992); David P. Szatmary, *A Time to Rock: A Social History of Rock 'n' Roll* (New York: Schirmer Books, 1996); Mark Gavreau Judge, *If It Ain't Got that Swing: The Rebirth of Grown-Up Culture* (New York: Spence, 2000); Cheryl L. Keyes, *Rap Music and Street Consciousness* (Urbana: University of Illinois Press, 2002); Peter Blecha, *Taboo Tunes: A History of Banned & Censored Songs* (San Francisco: Backbeat, 2004); and Simon Frith, *Popular Music: Critical Concepts in Media and Cultural Studies* (London: Routledge, 2004).

15. Robert Herrick, *Hesperides* (McMinnville, OR: Phillip J. Pirages Rare Books, 1648).

16. Kitty Ferguson, *The Music of Pythagoras: How an Ancient Brotherhood Cracked the Code of the Universe and Lit the Path from Antiquity to Outer Space* (New York: Walker and Company, 2008). See also Jamie James, *The Music of the Spheres: Music, Science, and the Natural Order of the Universe* (New York: Springer, 1993).

17. See Theodor Adorno, *Beethoven: The Philosophy of Music; Fragments and Texts* (Cambridge: Polity Press, 1993).

18. Greil Marcus, *Dead Elvis: A Chronicle of a Cultural Obsession* (New York: Anchor Books, 1991), p. 18.

6 The Kiss Goes to the Movies

1. Cited in Laura Citron, *A Compendium of Kisses* (New York: Harlequin, 2011), p. 76. See also André Gaudreault and Germain Lacasse, "The Introduction of the Lumière Cinematograph in Canada," *Canadian Journal of Film Studies* 5 (1996): 112–123, for an overview of the effect of Edison's new technology on social change.

2. Jean-Luc Godard, *Projections* (London: Faber and Faber, 1992), p. 8.

3. Cited in John Berger, *Sense of Sight* (New York: Vintage, 1993), p. 12.

4. Timothy Knight, *Great Kisses and Famous Lines Right Out of the Movies* (New York: It Books, 2008).

5. Richard J. Harris, Fred W. Sanborn, Christina L. Scott, Laura A. Dodds, and Jason D. Brandenberg, "Autobiographical Memories for Seeing Romantic Movies on a Date: Romance Is Not Just for Women," *Media Psychology* 6 (2004): 257–284.

6. Emily W. Leider, *Dark Lover: The Life and Death of Rudolph Valentino* (New York: Farrar, Straus and Giroux, 2003).

7. David Baird, *Captivating Couples: Celebrating Love on the Silver Screen* (London: MQ Publications, 2005), p. 9.

8. In-depth analyses of the social effects of *Greed* can be found in Joel W. Finler, *Greed: A Film* (New York: Lorimer, 1971) and Richard Koszarski, *The Man You Love to Hate: Erich von Stroheim and Hollywood* (Oxford: Oxford University Press, 1983).

9. See Sheldon Hall and Stephen Neale, *Epics, Spectacles, and Blockbusters: A Hollywood History* (Detroit: Wayne State University Press, 2010).

10. Marcel Danesi, *X-Rated: The Power of Mythic Symbolism in Popular Culture* (New York: Palgrave Macmillan, 2008).

11. Mark I. Pinsky, *The Gospel according to Disney: Faith, Trust, and Pixie Dust* (Louisville: Westminster John Knox Press, 2004), p. 77.

12. James C. Robertson, *The Casablanca Man: The Cinema of Michael Curtiz* (London: Routledge, 1993).

7 The Kiss in the Internet Age

1. Sheril Kirshenbaum, *The Science of Kissing: What Our Lips Are Telling Us* (New York: Grand Central, 2011), p. 59.

2. Jean Baudrillard, *Simulations* (New York: Semiotexte, 1983).

3. Linda M. Scott, *Fresh Lipstick: Redressing Fashion and Feminism* (New York: Palgrave, 2005), p. 166.

4. Manuel Castells, *The Internet Galaxy* (Oxford: Oxford University Press, 2001).

5. See Marshall McLuhan, *Understanding Media* (London: Routledge & Kegan Paul, 1964).

6. Arjun Appadurai, *Modernity at Large: Cultural Dimensions of Globalization* (Minneapolis: University of Minnesota Press, 1996).

7. Lori Andrews, *I Know Who You Are and I Saw What You Did: Social networks and the Death of Privacy* (New York: Free Press, 2012), p. 56.

8. Studies of online dating and the expression of emotions in cyberspace are proliferating, indicating that the shift to cyberspace for romantic expression is now the norm. See, for example, Aaron Ben Ze'ev, *Love Online: Emotions on the Internet* (Cambridge: Cambridge University Press, 2004) and Arvid Kappas and Nicole C. Krämer (eds.), *Face-to-Face Communication over the*

Internet: Emotions in a Web of Culture, Language, and Technology (Cambridge: Cambridge University Press, 2011).

9. Cristina Nehring, *A Vindication of Love: Reclaiming Romance for the Twenty-First Century* (New York: HarperCollins, 2009).

10. Alfred Kinsey, *Sexual Behavior in the Human Male* (Bloomington: Indiana University Press, 1948) and Alfred Kinsey, *Sexual Behavior in the Human Female* (Bloomington: Indiana University Press, 1953).

11. Magnus Hirschfeld, *Men and Women: The World Journey of a Sexologist* (New York: AMS Press, 1933).

12. Bronislaw Malinowski, *Sex and Repression in Savage Society* (London: Routledge & Kegan Paul, 1927) and Margaret Mead, *Sex and Temperament in Three Primitive Societies* (New York: Perennial, 1936).

13. Ernest Crawley, *Primitive Marriage and Its System* (Kila, MT: Kessinger Publications Reprint, 2005).

14. Carey Wilson and Wendy Hill, "Affairs of the Lips: Why We Kiss," *Scientific American Mind,* February 2008, 23–46.

15. Much of the relevant research is discussed by Kirshenbaum, *The Science of Kissing.*

16. Susan M. Hughes, Marissa A. Harrison, and Gordon G. Gallup, Jr., "Sex Differences in Romantic Kissing among College Students: An Evolutionary Perspective," *Evolutionary Psychology* 5 (2007): 612–631.

17. Donna Freitas, *The End of Sex* (New York: Basic Books, 2013).

18. Emma Goldman, *Anarchism and Other Essays* (London: Fifield, 1910), p. 23.

19. Kirshenbaum, *The Science of Kissing,* p. 209.

Index

Printed in Great Britain
by Amazon